Pro Man Woman
The Pro Man Guide For The Modern Woman

SHANDA FREEMAN

Copyright © 2014 Shanda Freeman

Publishing Consultant Diva Enterprise Books

All rights reserved.

ISBN: 0989393143
ISBN-13: 978-0989393140

DEDICATION

To the first man I ever loved, my stepfather,
Leroy P. Webb. I'm so grateful to have had you in my
life. You were a constant pillar of support and guidance.
You fostered my strengths and believed in my abilities
way before I did. I pray I continue to make you and
mommy proud.

OVERVIEW

Shanda gives a frank and humorous view into the male perspective. It is her version of the "Male Bible!" Men will love her take on everything women need to hear! Women will love her for her openness and honesty! It is a sexy, humorous and intelligent look into Love, Intimacy, and Relationships that both sexes will appreciate and enjoy!.

CONTENTS

	Preface	1
	Introduction	3
1	Separate We're Together	11
2	A.D.D.	21
3	Keeping Up With The Benjamin's	31
4	Let's Get It On	42
5	Head Games	57
6	Love Is All We Need	67
7	Handle With Care	77
8	We Are Family	89
9	Because I'm Happy	100
10	The Truth Of The Matter	111
11	Wait A Minute	121

PREFACE

"It isn't what I do, but how I do it. It isn't what I say, but how I say it, and how I look when I do it and say it."
– Mae West

Men. My weakness. My Kryptonite. I've had a love affair of men my whole life. What they think, how they feel, what they desire, what they wish for. As a woman I've always appreciated the male opinion. Sexually, Intellectually and Emotionally.
What does a man really want?
What is he not getting that he needs?
What does he need from me as a woman?
In learning who I am as a woman, I had to acknowledge the male influence. In my journey, I've found that men in general are very simplistic. There are just certain things they need and certain things they don't want. The shit that drives them crazy, in good and bad ways of course! The issue for many men has been that for too long too many books have been written by women about what they're lacking, what they need to do, or what they're doing wrong.

Where is the love from a woman that appreciates and acknowledges their thoughts, feelings and actions? Well, loves your girl is here! As a woman, it was important for me to offer a platform for men to be appreciated, understood and acknowledged. This ain't a "We are from different planets, I hate what men do point of view!" This is all love baby!! From Sex and Intimacy, to Communication and Finances, this book will challenge women and their views on matters regarding men and what they can do to better their relationships.

It's a sex and relationship guide unlike any other that allows men to say all the things they wish they could say to their woman but are hesitant to. Most men don't want to deal with the drama that comes with bringing up certain subjects regarding what he wants or needs from his woman. Now, I'm going to say off top, this is not a book about submission and being subservient. It's about love, appreciation and yes, my personal favorite, gratification!

INTRODUCTION

"Shanda, you love men!" If I had a dollar for every time I was told that, I'd be a very rich woman! So, why this love affair of men? To be honest, I've always loved the male presence. Since a young girl I had crushes and was batting my eyes and admiring boys. I can remember being in Kindergarten and liking boys so my fascination and appreciation started very early! But, truthfully if I had to really look at the heart of it, it would be my stepfather. He was a wonderful man, and in thinking back I realized he taught me so much in who I am as a woman and as a person.

He honestly took a more active role in shaping who I am, more so than my mother. And not to take anything away from her, he was just more hands on and more communicative with me than she was. Over time I learned to value his opinion greatly and in turn wanting to always please him because he valued mine and showed a genuine interest in me emotionally.

He was very influential in inspiring me and motivating me. Loving and appreciating a man comes natural to me. It's like breathing. Now, I'm not going to say that I haven't been on the right side of wrong with a man, of course I have. But innately I am more a lover than a fighter. I enjoy taking care of a man and spoiling him. I love making love and yes I love fucking too! To me they're two different expressions. We'll talk about that later. But, I'm very passionate. Lustful. Sexual. I'm proud of that.

As a confident woman, I embrace it. I've found that men appreciate my openness and my ability to see past my sex when it comes to love and intimacy. I've always been fascinated by the male opinion and quite honestly I've found that many women don't think or care much about it. My feeling has always been, if you want a good man and if you want a relationship or marriage that's meaningful, why not listen to what he's asking or at least entertain it?

In listening you hear everything you need to know. But how many of us women really listen to what a man needs and better yet, see him for who he truly is and not what we wish him to be? I've found that men find it very profound when a woman takes the time to care and pay attention in getting to know HIM. Being able to be heard and appreciated is reciprocal. Women often times get into a mindset that as a man you need to do this, you need to do that, but men have longings and emotions that need to be met as well. It's not all about making a woman happy. There has to be a general appreciation and generosity between the two.

As women, we can often times take on the "generational tone" in our relationships. How we've seen our mothers and grandmothers behave and how they react to men and relationships can either inspire us or harden us towards men. It's like that old adage' "children learn what they live." The same holds true in what we see and what we've lived through, through the women around us. For myself, I come from a strong opinionated woman! My mom was tough. She was a no holds barred, don't cross me, I'm not having it type of woman and for every one thing my stepfather gave her, she gave it back twofold. So my experiences were seeing her take no shit. Ever.

As a young girl I always looked at her as a rock. Solid. If I were to be honest with you, I can't say I always admired it. I felt that she was so tough that it was hard to see her softness. Again, my mother had taken on the tone of who my grandmother was. There is a lot to be said about a woman who stands up for herself. I admire that. But, there are moments in our lives that we're so motivated by anger and pain that we forget to be soft and gentle.

We only know to protect ourselves while shutting others out. It can be challenging for a man trying to love a woman who has so much pain cloaked around her that he can't get through to her heart and who she truly is. I've been there. When you've been hurt and your trust has been compromised it's very easy to become impenetrable. But, what begins to happen is every man gets to wear that same cloak of anger, insecurity and frustration that the previous man gave you.

At what point do you let all that go and allow yourself to enjoy love and allow yourself to be loved? One of the biggest gifts I gave myself was accepting accountability. Meaning, in looking back in my past relationships I had to accept blame where it was due. I had to accept that hey, you could have done this. You could have been better in this aspect. I had to admit that I made mistakes.

I had to admit that I wasn't perfect and quite honestly, admit that I was with someone that I knew deep down was not for me. And in admitting that, I had to ask myself why? Why am I with someone who I know is not for me? Who's not respecting me? Who's not growing with me? Why am I staying? We make a choice every day in co-signing our relationships whether good or bad. If you stay in these "treadmill type" of relationships and you're hurting, why?

Accountability forces us to look at ourselves in the mirror and examine why we feel we don't deserve better. How as a woman can you get to a place that you love a man openly and without reservation? How do you get to a place where all the things that I'm sharing in this book that it feels right to do so?

First, and foremost and I'm sure many of you have heard it before is LOVING yourself. And it sounds so cliché. But, it's one of the realest statements and facts. You CANNOT love another person without having a true knowledge of loving yourself. Think of it this way, it's like inviting company over and your home is dirty. You have to clean house before you go inviting someone in!

We honestly have to take a more ACTIVE role in loving ourselves. The action is being responsible in everyday affirmation. We have to practice it. Not just talk about it. I say this because many of us know our insecurities. As women we can openly share them with other women in admitting we don't love ourselves enough and we let things that are important to us and ourselves go.

We admit it's easier taking care of other people than ourselves. We allow ourselves to wallow and become just a sounding board of pain and regret. Part of being a grown ass man or woman is accepting our issues. Part of loving ourselves is recognizing those issues and doing something about them so that we can allow love to happen.

I was having a deep conversation with a male friend of mine. We were discussing relationships of course, and he was explaining to me the type of relationships and women he always seems to be attracted to. He admitted he wasn't always happy about it or proud of his choices or behavior.

During the conversation he says, "Shan, this is what it is, this is how I am." So, I let him finish saying what he had to say. Let him fully express himself and at the end of it, I said "This is bullshit." Y'all know the look he gave me right? But, I said it was bullshit because if you can sit and tell me all your wrongs and you're fully aware of them then why just say 'it's who I am?' If you know it's not right and it's not good for you then as an adult, you can change them!

It's a choice you make. Either you want better and want to do better or you just keep repeating the same crap over and over. Let's keep the honesty flowing. How many of us want to keep repeating a negative? It's like never getting over a cold. You're always sick. Ain't nobody got time for that! At some point we got to put our big panties on and get a life. For many of us our past and upbringing keeps us in the negative when it comes to having a meaningful relationship. And this is not a man or woman thing it's a shared issue.

You have to let go of the past to claim your future. It's tough. It's not an easy road and letting it go does not mean that you're forgetting it. Think of how many times we've heard that statement. "Let it go. Let it go." But, it's a plain truth. I'm going to share this with you. There have been many instances in my life, that my past by all accounts could have claimed my future. There are very personal events that have happened to me that quite frankly should have soured me. Events that had ultimately affected my relationships.

As strong as I am today, I wasn't always. In looking back I wish I could have rewritten things. But the reality is life goes in its direction to teach us lessons. It's not always pretty but to grow it is what it is and often times what has to happen. The key is not allowing it to take our ability to have decent lives and have relationships and marriages that are meaningful and lasting.

To many of us the concept is foreign and may even feel intangible. For myself, I had to get over anger. Many things that have happened had me in a state of always been on the defense. I always was ultra sensitive and it's a trait that I still have to be very aware of to this day. I'm very sensitive and as great as that can be in some respects it can also be sabotaging.

I've had to learn to just let things flow and not to take things so personal at times and also let the man in my life know that at the end of it all, I trust him. Allowing yourself to give your trust is paramount in loving another person. And yall know to give that is not easy. But for some, their trust is handed over on silver platters to those that have not earned it.

We have to be accountable in that respect because we have to allow others to grow with us and prove that they should have our complete trust. We women are very good at opening ourselves like a book with our trust and our hearts. We want so much to be happy and to be loved and yes, to be trusted that we freely give all those attributes often times to men we've barely known three months. We all have been guilty of that.

I will tell you, when a man sees you give so much so quickly it's a red flag to him. He may not openly say it, but one or two things may happen. Either he will run with it and take advantage of you. Or he may pull way back because he's feeling your moving too fast and giving so much. It's scary to him. He's nowhere near how you're feeling emotionally and he's feeling like you have issues and he's not trying to get caught up in all that. Our trust just like our love and our bodies has to be earned.

A good man, the right man will respect that. He will admire you for it. He will view you differently because he sees you as being a woman who is responsible and respects herself above all things. And how we treat ourselves and what we allow from the very beginning sets the tone in how others view us. It's about self respect. If you have that, it shines through and people will see that a mile away. You enter a room and people feel the energy that you give that lets them know, this is a woman of class, substance, and respect.

What you are is what you attract. Really absorb that. How you carry yourself and how you present yourself sets a tone for how others will treat and perceive you. In finding a good man, that you feel comfortable doing all these things that I share with you, you have to be a good woman. You have to. And there is nothing subservient or submissive about that. That's a lesson that I had to learn. Me just admitting that I wanted to be a good woman for a man, it initially felt like I had to compromise who I am and my beliefs. But in maturing and through life experience I realized it is a beautiful and just feeling. That it's ok for me to admit that I want to be good to a man. It makes me happy to do so. And that doesn't mean that I have to be perfect and that I have to run in circles to keep him happy.

It just means that my "house" is clean and I'm ready and prepared for "company." In my love for men, over the years I've realized that in my mind I've always held them to a standard. Based on who my stepfather was as a man and my relationship with him. He allowed me to embrace that men are not an enemy, but the right man a source of comfort, respect, and love that no woman could ever give me.

My ideal of men was not always represented well in my choices but I take accountability for that because they were my choices. But, I've been blessed to not be soured or turned off by experiences. My choices and past haven't sullied my respect and love for men. Now, there are some men in my life that don't leave a pleasant memory for me but I take the good with the bad. But, I also take what my choices have taught me. How they've allowed me to grow as a woman and as a loving woman.

I'm appreciative of all the lessons. In moving forward and sharing this book with you the greatest gift I can give you is this: Allow every negative experience to teach you. Allow every bad choice to guide you to know better next time and don't let it tarnish you in thinking there is not a man out there that fits you perfectly and deserves what I share with you.

My promise to myself? That for the next man in my life, he will be my greatest effort. Meaning all my mistakes, everything that I could have done better, I'll do better. Every issue I've accepted and addressed that he gets the best of me. He gets my greatest accomplishment, the best of what I know love to be emotionally and physically. That's exciting to me!

It's with that excitement and enthusiasm that I ask you to read this with an open heart, open mind, and open arms. It will at times, as a woman, challenge your beliefs and emotions in how you view men. Most of what I share is through personal experience but the gist of what I'm sharing is through countless interviews with men and their thoughts and feelings regarding women and relationships.

You're getting it from the horse's mouth so to speak. It isn't always pretty but as a writer, I love that it comes from a place of honesty and no reserve. Again, we as women can learn a lot of what men need through what they have to say. As a Pro Man woman, Let's hear it from the boys!

CHAPTER 1
SEPARATE WE'RE TOGETHER

Love creates an 'us' without destroying a 'me'.
- Leo Buscaglia

Ladies, I tell you, when a man gets up in your nostrils, he can drive a truck through them! The beginning stages of a relationship have always been a very exciting time for me. I love spoiling a man! Stimulating his mind and his body is a huge high for me. I've gotten so caught up in this reverie of lust and excitement that I will forget everything and everyone just to be in this world of "The King and I".

I have very often started my relationships this way and though it's very satisfying in the beginning stages, it can go left at any moment. You know the saying holds true in how we begin our relationships will set the tone on how our relationships play out. I have ALWAYS been guilty of establishing my life around my man.

Let me share with you one of my "light bulb" moments. A particular ex of mine, whom I shall not name, said to me one day "Babe, don't you have something to do?" Now, in that moment, two things could have happened. I could have shriveled up and waited for a hole to appear in the floor for me to fall into or I could have cussed him out and proceeded to hand him his ass, since I had waited on him hand and foot all day. But, I'll tell you what your girl did.

I took that and I LISTENED. I honestly didn't get angry. Though inside I was hurt, I didn't let him see it. The truth was I NEEDED to hear that because quite frankly in looking back I was smothering him. Without even noticing it, all the things I use to do, I literally stopped doing. Going out with my girlfriends, going to the gym, even small things like my reading. I use to read two to three novels at a time and I had even cut back on doing that.

It hit me one day that I hadn't read in months and that's when I got pissed. At myself. Again, this was a choice I made and let parts of me go to the wayside in order to feed my relationship. And let me be clear. There has never been any man that I loved that made me do anything that I didn't wish to do. Every bit of spoiling I did because I wanted to. My "attention to detail" and always wanting to please kept me in this place. I don't look at it as a bad thing in retrospect. I just had to learn to balance myself physically and emotionally. Meaning this is what I give "him" and this is what I give "me" and one doesn't eliminate the other. I had to learn this through my mistakes because there is no better teacher than someone telling you what it is.

I'll be honest with you this is an aspect of men that I love. The give it to me straight, in a no chaser and no bullshit kind of way. I appreciate honesty from a man. Even if the truth hurts me. I can operate from a place of truth. In doing so I've realized every great relationship starts with the ability for the individuals to stay individuals.

It is imperative that each person maintains a life of self-accomplishment, independence and interests that are separate from the relationship. It alleviates the need for one partner having to serve all the needs of the other.

Think of the kind of pressure that puts on an individual to have to supply all your needs. It's unfair and it starts the beginning of resentment and alienation. As partners you have to be able to motivate each other. You have to both feel free and encouraged in reaching your full potentials. I motivate you. You motivate me. It keeps you both in a place of consistent growth and maturity.

Think of why people are so enamored by Jay Z and Beyonce's marriage. They appear to the world to have a great balance of independence and success as individuals and as a couple they are stronger as a result. She hasn't asked him to change who he is and he hasn't asked her to give up who she is because they're married. They are allowing each other to be the best of themselves and it's something we all wish to obtain.

I'm going to share with you another area where I had to check myself. I was one of those types of women that was a Cling-on. Meaning, I can be around my man all day, asking him "Honey are you ok?" Do you need anything? Are you hungry baby? My behavior was what I call, "a gnat at a cookout" I had this thing with me that I always needed to ask questions and not leave my man to himself. I cannot begin to tell you how many men that are in a relationship shared with me that they wish their women would get that they just want to be left ALONE.

What was so funny for me was sitting through these interviews and seeing myself guilty as charged. I was always up my man's ass. So when the subject of 'alone' came up, I was open because I knew this was one of the things I needed to understand. A woman's initial reaction is, "Alone? What you mean? How you gonna be "alone" in a relationship?" These are all questions that we women come to in our defense when our man says he just wants to be left "alone." It can bring on feelings of anger and rejection. It puts us on instant defense. "Then be by your damned self!" Is a popular response to this "alone" subject!

But, in being left alone, what was expressed was that as men they needed to have part of themselves that belongs to them. Not their woman, not their kids, just him. And being alone doesn't mean that anything is wrong. It just means, what it means. There's a reason why men need a "man cave" in their home. It's that get away from everything and everybody where he gets to do man shit. Whatever that is. Listen, even Batman had the Bat Cave! Another "poignant" subject that was brought up was, silence. Now, not all men are quiet. I've been with very talkative men. But silence in the aspect of they just don't need to talk as much.

Now, I'm a Gemini, and if you know astrology, you know that we are the communicators of the zodiac. I'm always communicating. Always asking questions and wanting to constantly learn and understand behaviors. So, in my marriage there were times that I realized I really just needed to accept the silence.

Here's a gem I want to share with you ladies. When a man is comfortable enough to be around you without a lot of talking, it's a compliment. Him letting you in his space lets you know he trusts you to be there. Silence is considered golden. He may not say much, but his ACTIONS will speak volumes.

As women we have to trust in that and not question everything. What I've learned over the years is that as women we take our feelings regarding love and communication and we multiply it by 10! Men are much more simplistic with it. I have this analogy. Women are like the novel War and Peace. Men are Cliff Notes. We take shit to a whole other level that it does not need go. Learning and accepting this is huge because it allows you the freedom of letting go and just relax. Everything's good. Nothing is wrong. No need to sound the alarms. It's funny and you have to look at it in a humorous way. But, in truth the ability to set ourselves apart really allows for a closer relationship.

Men have expressed to me that the woman that allows him his space and also values hers, is the one that's special. He views her differently because she's not about compromising all of who she is for the relationship. So, how do you get to a place of separation? For one, you have to keep yourself busy. Big lesson I learned. You can't be constantly thinking and obsessing about him, if you have things you're doing that are important to you.

What are your hobbies and interests? What goals have you set for yourself that you haven't started on or accomplished fully as yet? Have you even set goals for yourself regarding professional or personal fulfillment? Also, are you spending time with your family and friends, without your man?

You don't have to go everywhere and do everything together. An important piece here to remember is your friends and family were in your life prior to your marriage or relationship and that shouldn't be compromised because of it. You have to maintain your friendships individually. Think of how important it is in giving yourself space and escape. And I don't mean that in an extravagant way. Meaning, it's important to have those close friend and family relationships that when you need to talk or just feel like you need to get away from him, the kids, whatever, you have that outlet and space to go to. It's necessary.

I maintain a very close relationship with family and a few friends that I trust because it helps to balance me. My home is also a place of escape for my friends and family as well so it's very important you have those connections and keep them no matter your relationship or marriage status. Now, let's talk the phone and texting issue. Let me ask you, how many times a day do you text your man or call him? And when you do what kind of response do you receive? Nine times out of ten it's not as elaborate as yours is it? It's a yes or no response or it's a response that you may feel doesn't have the right amount of emotions in it? Or their response comes back later than you appreciate, which puts you in detective mode. Big thing here, men are not texters. They don't like being on the phone for long periods of time. Unless of course they're talking about money, fucking, or getting more money. That's just what it is. They're not going to do all the extra we do. And it doesn't mean that they care any less. You can't take it personal. It's just is what it is.

For myself, I always in need of these certain responses in my phone calls and texts. Those I miss you's and I love you's. Always looking for my affirmations. I was always texting, "Do you miss me? Did you think about me today, babe?" We women are often times expecting these responses every time. But, this is where our trust comes into play.

If you have a good man that loves and supports you just trust in that. The trust allows you to go on and do you. It allows you to free your mind and let go of the insecurity that comes with constantly aligning yourself to your partner. Here's another gem I want to share with you ladies and I really need you to take this in because this is some TRUTH for your ass right here! EVERY TIME that I would go out with my girls, or do a weekend visit with family or friends and I wouldn't communicate much, I would get more attention than if I were around my man all day! He would be blowing up my phone and asking, what you doing? Hope you're having fun? When you coming home? I honestly would chuckle to myself and say, "Yeah, I got yo ass now!" It doesn't take a genius to figure it out really. The less you give them, the more they want and need from you. And not that it's a game, because really it isn't. It's honestly about allowing that freedom of thought and wonder and even chase that a man needs in his woman. When we surrender that chase we become boring and predictable, and that's the kiss of death to many a relationship and marriage. Your man has to see you get along just fine without him. He needs those, "I wonder what her ass is doin', I ain't heard from her all day!"

thoughts. You gotta keep him on his toe's ladies! You have to be able to get yo life!

Now, let's talk about what I call "Housewife Syndrome." I want to preface this and tell you that this comes from a place of true experience from myself and I could not write this chapter without honestly addressing this issue. Being a housewife is an honorable task. I say this because I did it for over 10 years. Raising children, having a husband and keeping your home flowing and everyone relying on and needing you to hold them down as a mom and wife is a huge responsibility.

I don't take anything away from it. It's not a job that every woman is cut out for so the one's that do it and do it well are due the utmost honor and respect. What often times can happen, and it did happen to me, was all my life was, was just that. My husband and my children. I cannot begin to tell you the countless amount of friends that I have, who are housewives, who appear to have it all, but are empty inside. Empty because they're not fulfilling their own personal goals and accomplishments.

As noted earlier, I spoke about how important it is as individuals that we have that. It's very difficult to be innately happy when your husband provides everything. You can have the best shoes, bags, expensive cars, and beautiful home that he provides for you, but it still will not be enough if you're not servicing your individuality in a way that empowers YOU. You honestly begin to become so dependent that you can't even remember what your goals and dreams were for yourself anymore. This can be a dangerous place for a woman to be in and here is where you have to establish your voice.

You have to share with your husband how important it is for you to do something that allows you to feel good about yourself aside of what he provides for you. Also, don't feel guilt about this. It's very hard as a woman sometimes to come to terms with putting your dreams and goals on the table for yourself because we feel that it may sacrifice our children or marriage in some way. And I won't sugar coat it, in some ways it can. But, there is nothing more profound than finding your voice and allowing your independence in your relationship.

In doing my interviews I found that the majority of men, WANT a woman who has her own personal and professional goals. No, he's not intimidated or threatened by it but honestly respects it and appreciates it. We are in a day and age that more and more men respect that independent woman spirit and quite frankly are turned off more by a woman that has no goals for herself. They want and appreciate a woman that has a voice and can hold her own.

Any man that can hold down his home and allow his children and wife to live in a way that he's proud of deserves the ultimate respect. Men work very hard for their families to have the best. But, you have to understand that all the material things and comfort that that comes with cannot fill a void that only you can provide for yourself. As a couple you have to communicate and respect each other's respective goals and compromise on how to move forward and what's best as a family.

There was a time that I had all those things, but I didn't have myself and it was a very lonely place for me. So, I share this with you in hopes that as a "couple" you empower and support each other. You allow yourselves the gift of working on your dreams and aspirations and not work from a place of jealousy or covetousness but of continual support and guidance and helping each other be the best that you both can be individually.

A couple that knows how to create that balance will be happier and in turn allow the relationship to flourish and grow in a deeper and more impactful way. There is nothing more beautiful than two people that allow the betterment of each other while maintaining individual success. That's a bond that no one can break and that's priceless!

CHAPTER 2
A.D.D.
(ATTENTIVE DEFICIT DISORDER)

"A woman should soften but not weaken a man."

-Sigmund Freud

For every man dealing with a "Cling-on" woman, there are twenty more who are bored and lonely in their relationships. Attentive Deficit Disorder is my definition of the FORGOTTEN MAN. Living on a time clock of expectation and predictability, he is in a no man's land of constant frustration and tension with no release. A man filled with numerous regrets and reverie. With memories of the past, he daydreams of a life of passion, lust and spontaneity.

Really Shanda? Yes, Really! This is the part where you can laugh! I know that sounded very melodramatic, but it's VERY REAL so listen up! Let's start at the beginning. For one, it's important to acknowledge your man's presence in YOUR life. Take away the kids, the financial responsibility, everything other than you and him. Look at your relationship on a one on one basis. If you had to view your man through another person's eyes what would you see?

Here's one better. If you were to view him through ANOTHER WOMAN'S eyes, what do you think SHE sees? What does she see that maybe you've turned a blind eye to? Are you affectionate, attentive? Are you servicing his needs sexually and intimately? Are you supportive of him emotionally as well as professionally? Let's start at the beginning. Before we go deep into this chapter, I don't want you ladies flaring your nose up, sucking your teeth and getting defensive.

Yes, I acknowledge that we as women struggle with these same issues at times, but this ain't about us right now. This is about us accepting our role and responsibility in making our men feel happy and fulfilled. I want to say from the jump, I don't believe as a woman it is our sole responsibility to make our man happy. There are certain things only he can provide for himself. That's a given. But, if I can be honest with you, I cannot begin to tell you how many men at my job would divulge their private thoughts with me regarding their relationships.

In doing my research and interviews one of the biggest concerns shared with me was the lack of ACKNOWLEDGEMENT. They don't often feel appreciated. Everything that's done is expected. The attitude is "As a man, this is what you supposed to be doing." And yes, in looking at the roles of men and women, there is some definite truth to that. I know that as a woman, there are just certain things that I look to a man to bring to the table. But, ladies the good ones acknowledge this as well. The disconnect comes in when we forget to be supportive, appreciative and communicative about the role he plays in your life.

I think a key factor many of us women don't realize is that in general men are bolstered by our acknowledgment and appreciation. When you can openly express your feelings about how much you love and respect what he does and provides for you it empowers him! I believe it's so important to empower your man because he looks to you for that. Think of it this way, would you like him getting it from another woman? It's our responsibility to do so. "Wait, did she just say it's our responsibility?" I know some of you think I'm tripping, but yes, you read that correctly. I said it's our RESPONSIBILITY. If he is getting in your bed at night, entering your body, and sharing your life with you, then why is it hard to accept that it's a RESPONSIBILITY? For every woman who has her nose flared reading this, I'm going to tell you why you feel the way you do. Because it sounds like it's your job. It may even sound subservient in some aspects. Your instant reflex is I don't have to do shit. The reality is you don't. You don't have to do anything you don't wish to do. But, here's the flip to that. For every bit of acknowledgement you feel you deserve, why isn't he allowed the same courtesy? For every bit of respect you demand, he deserves it as well. We women want and expect these things from our men. It's only right to return what we wish for as well and there's nothing submissive or subservient about that. It's what's right. We have to get off our high horse about us being number one. "I'm mommy, I'm wife, I'm holding everybody down." There's lots of truth in that. But, if your man is handling his business he deserves that spot right next to you on that pedestal. The blurred lines come in when we get into our own feelings and can't see past ourselves. Your need for acknowledgement in what you bring to the table cannot overshadow your need to be reciprocal. As couples, it's important to identify and accept that what we each bring to our relationships is unique and just. We have to be in sync with how we communicate our appreciation and respect for each other. Don't allow your pride to get in the way of being humble with your man. Humility is a forgotten asset. Humility is often mistaken as submission. Saying thank you and allowing yourself to be thankful is moral. There is no shame in that. Now, I want to bring up a subject that many men feel real guilt over. Children. In acknowledging the "elephant in the room" many men have admitted that once their children entered their lives, their relationships changed. Admittedly, children can play a huge role in the disconnect of many couples. It happens very easily and often silently. When you become parents, it's a natural process for you to put your children first. Once that child enters your lives the roles of priorities change. All your love and attention goes into these little people. As a mother, and the responsibilities that it comes with, it's so easy to give our children all of our attention, affection, and time. But we have to be very careful in balancing our attention and efforts. We have to remember that our "first baby" still needs and wants his attention and affection as well.

Put, it this way, they were his titties first! The reality is that our responsibility as parents can easily overshadow our relationships. I always challenge couples to have an agreement. It's something my mother shared with me and I pass it on to you. As a couple from the very beginning, you have to both agree that there is no one person, place or thing that is bigger than you as a UNIT. That includes your children. Now, I know many of us are brought up with the belief that our children come first, but it is my opinion they do not. Let me explain. As a couple, the glue to it all is your RELATIONSHIP. I cannot stress this enough. You have to understand that your passion, lust, friendship, appreciation, respect and love for each other is PRIORITY.

Your children do not come before that. If these principles are put on the back burner then the breakdown slowly begins. There is a beauty and comfort that comes with this. It's what I like to refer to as the "Safety Zone." When life gets crazy or unfair, when your kids get out of control, our whatever the challenges are, your safety is that bond that you share with each other. That bond has to be serviced and catered to and can never be made to feel that it is not a priority. By either of you. I have been married twice and what I've learned over time and experience is that men, though they may not communicate their feelings as openly as we wish them to, have a great need to be loved and appreciated. They hate rejection.

They have to know that they can always count on you for that love, understanding, and intimacy. Your arms have to always be open AND your legs as well! Now, I'm sure that I probably just knocked you for a loop. But there need to be intimate and sexual is just as great, and over time because life and circumstances can get in the way, this particular aspect of your relationship may be one of the first to subside. Men love sex. As a woman I admit I do too. I can easily have sex more than once a day, and every day of the week for that matter. I am probably not the norm. But, so many men feel that sex is no longer a priority to their women anymore.

When there is a lack of interest and unwillingness to be engaged sexually by either partner, watch the shit to hit the fan. This is like a hole in the dike for relationships. I cannot stress enough how important it is for women to acknowledge their man's needs sexually. I proudly wave the flag for men in this area! Let's take the gloves off. If you show a lack of interest or are no longer servicing your man what do you honestly think he's supposed to do?

Now, there can be numerous legitimate reasons, why a woman is no longer engaged sexually. Health reasons, an emotional event and yes even her career can get in the way of having a profound intimate relationship with her man. But, what I will say is that for whatever reason there is, it has to be addressed. Swiftly. It cannot be ignored. You cannot leave your man out to pasture over an extended amount of time for any reason. The issues regarding sex and intimacy have to be discussed. Plain and simple. You both have to have the conversation.

It's not always easy and for many men it's very

uncomfortable. They often feel like they appear selfish if they express how they really feel if the lack of sex is a legitimate one. They also hate having to deal with the nasty ass attitude and look you give when he asks for some. How bad do you think he wants it now, if he has to put up with that kind of stink attitude and the "I'm tired and have a headache" excuse? And forget even asking for head!! That's like Hiroshima up in the bedroom!! All of it is such a turn off emotionally and physically. Real talk? Sex is important.

For every person reading this and believes that it's not, you're fooling yourself. Sex is a beautiful bonding experience for couples and when that bond is no longer being addressed by you, please believe it may be addressed by someone else. Is it right? No, but it's truth. As a woman, I'm going to lay it out there. If you show a lack of continual interest in your man sexually and you refuse to do anything about it, you cannot go running the New York marathon, Maury Show sprint when you find out, he's fuckin' someone else. Yeah, I said it. You have to be honest with yourself and acknowledge your role and accountability if that happens.

A person can only go for so long without physical and emotional support. No I do not condone cheating. But, I am a realist and I acknowledge the fact that these things can play a huge factor. The lack of sex and intimacy creates anger and resentment for men. A pent up man is not a good look for a man. Or a woman for that matter. I had to throw that in there!

There is no worse feeling than getting in bed at night wanting to make love and your partner acts like it's not important to them, turning their back to you and falling asleep. They know you want some! I have plenty of female friends that use sex as a weapon with their man, and quite honestly, I don't respect that. If you're one of those women, you need to stop this destructive behavior because it's unfair.

Sex should never be used as a form of revenge, punishment or a means of control. A person will only take so much of that kind of manipulation. Can I tell you, I've always been the type of woman that when I'm upset with my man, I want sex with him more so! It sounds crazy right? But, for me sex calms me and makes me happy. "Because I'm Happy!!" (Que Pharell) It takes away my anger so I can take my ass to sleep and then I'm good! But, bigger than my own happiness, as a woman I admit my man's sexual fulfillment is extremely important to me. I'm overly enthusiastic in regards to sex and to share another gem with you, I often will ask my man what he wants and have zero problems in giving it to him. I'm definitely an all in woman.

Ok, now wait. Let me back paddle here. What your girl won't be doing, is bringing in extras. This is not the WWF! I'm not tagging anybody in and ain't no ménage a trios going on! But as me and him go, I'm game! Again, in this area I feel it's a responsibility to make sure he's good. One thing about me, I never ever want my man to feel like he's missing out. I never want him to feel like I don't acknowledge his physical desires and needs. When he's on top, and yes I mean that figuratively I want him to feel like he's King! I love that. As a woman, don't feel ashamed or embarrassed if you enjoy allowing your man to be empowered this way. A satisfied man is a happy man for the most part. Let him beat his chest like Tarzan girl!!

As women we have to always be mindful how important his position is in our lives. It can never be taken for granted. As I stated earlier, life and circumstances can obstruct our importance to each other. Another big culprit here? Careers. Careers have the ability to always come first and everything and everyone else is secondary. There are many couples today who can contribute their careers as the downfall of their marriage or relationship. It stinks because as individuals we all wish to be accomplished. But with huge accomplishment often comes huge sacrifice.

I would be remiss in saying that it's easy. It's not. But, in coming from a very personal space in my last marriage, I always knew that my husband's career was his first love. It's not an easy thing to admit and quite frankly we had many arguments because of his commitment to it. But, to provide for his home and his family it is what's necessary. There is no easy answer here. And, here is where we go back to the "Safety Zone." When times like these are challenging and your careers are overwhelming you have to have that place that you honor for each other. That place where no one thing is bigger than the both of you. It's definitely going to challenge your relationships because how we provide is how we live and one cannot go without the other.

There's a saying, "Can a woman have it all?" Career, husband and children? I believe you can have it all. But, in having it all there will be sacrifices and in this book I refuse to gloss over any area. There will come days that you will have to choose between work and your husband, or work and your commitment to your children. There may be many things that you miss out on because you can't be everywhere doing everything for everybody. The money and the accomplishments are huge for us women because we've worked so hard to achieve them. We want that same level of respect and acknowledgment within our careers given to our male counterparts. Choosing between love and career is not easy and we've seen enough television shows centered around this very topic. But, in getting to the core of this subject, as a woman there is a lot we must take on if we sign up for the role as a wife or girlfriend.

I've always felt it very important that from the beginning it's essential to communicate with your man what your abilities and limitations are. It's not something many of us do, but in maturing I've realized how important it is to create realistic goals and even boundaries within your personal relationship with your man.

Some of us women are great at one thing and not so great in another area. I can cook and clean my ass off but I suck at laundry. I just hate doing it and I expressed that early. So, we sent our laundry out. We talked about it and we came to a solution about it. I know that's a trivial example but what I'm trying to convey is to always be open and honest with each other about what you can and can't do.

Don't ignore important issues and don't allow the elephant to take up space in your relationships. His ass should not be having a permanent seat on y'all's couch! Communication is vital in every aspect of your relationship. If you're unhappy say it. If you're unfulfilled don't be afraid to express it. If you're feeling ignored or unappreciated express that. Addressing these concerns early and coming to a compromise sooner than later allows your relationship to strengthen. Don't allow anything or anyone to become cancerous to your relationship and especially your marriage. I have personally experienced others being allowed to come in and destroy what took years to build. It is the worst feeling in the world and not something I ever wish anyone to go through. Again, there should be no one thing, or person bigger than the two of you.

In closing I want to say this. If someone you love is a priority and they're important to you, you'll do what you have to do. You'll make sure you've done your absolute best and give it your greatest effort. You will show up and show out. I know as a woman, I want a man that looks to me to be his baby. That he looks at me in a way that I'm irreplaceable. I want my man to always feel those butterflies and excitement in his heart and in his pants when he thinks about me. The excitement, passion, lust, friendship and respect that only I can provide for him.

Do not take your relationships and marriages for granted. Ask questions and be present. Never assume anything. Have those pillow talks and quiet moments with each other. Listen and be open to change if it's going to make your relationships stronger. Let your man know how important he is to you. Be his baby. His cheerleader. His confidante and his courtesan. I was gonna say the other word, but you know what I mean. Most importantly be his friend. That friendship and that bond will be the one thing you can always count on and the one thing no one else can give or take from either of you. Your Safety Zone.

CHAPTER 3
KEEPING UP WITH THE BENJAMIN'S

"With money you can buy a house, but not a home. With money you can buy a clock, but not time. With money you can buy a book, but not knowledge. With money you can buy blood, but not life. With money you can buy sex, but not love. So what can you buy with money???"- Prem Rawat

A man and his money are not soon parted! If there is one thing a man is serious about, is his money! Men are defined by their ability to earn. Not solely of course, but a man that has the ability to earn and provide well carries with him great pride and respect. As a woman, part of how we view a good man is based on this very concept. We may not always openly admit it, but having a man who is well established financially is a quality many of us women wish for.

There is a certain pride that comes with saying your man is wealthy and accomplished. What we must not forget is that that very pride can either be a blessing or a curse to our relationships. The marriage of love and money is not always an easy one for some and learning from the very beginning your boundaries as a couple is important. Communication is the biggest form of survival when it comes to money and love. I cannot stress enough how important it is for two people to be on the same page about their finances.

For the most part, many men feel pressured to be perfect in this area. What was often the shared concern is that women want so much, without being realistic in what they can really have. Looking at a man's capabilities in what you expect from him financially is important because it takes the pressure not only off of him but the relationship or marriage as a whole. Let's face it, in this day of excess and materialism, it is harder on men to keep all the balls in the air with their women and families. The cars, clothes, and the right schools are only the tip of the iceberg in looking at what many men have to contend with in keeping it all together.

The pressure to have it all leads a path of destruction for so many because the ability to have it "all" is not practical. As couples, the communication has to begin from the jump in how WE are going to handle our finances. What are we feasibly able to have and to take on at this moment? I expressed WE specifically, because there are many marriages and relationships where one person is handling this aspect of their relationship solely. That person is the one in control and making most if not all of the financial decisions. If this is an agreed upon commitment, it is still important for the other partner to always be fully aware of what your shared current financial landscape looks like and still be an active voice in how it is to grow.

That one person should never use this position as a means of control. This is a disgraceful way of being manipulative and powerful. Your partner should never feel that they have to be beholden to you or feel beneath you because of your responsibility in handling the finances. Either person cannot be in the dark about what is going on financially. You both have to have a clear understanding of what is yours, mine's and ours.

Together you have to discuss what is put away for savings, vacations and retirement. What is on your priority list as a couple and what is for down the road? I've always felt that couples who share these type of honest and frank discussions regarding money have fewer problems and less "surprises" down the road. Surprises are most likely derived from one person not knowing what's fully going on, and by the time it gets to them it's when shit has already hit the fan!

The topic and discussion of money is difficult for some because the reality is not all of us are great at managing or saving it. Many of us have not even been taught how to handle money properly. The topic in and of itself can be a cause of embarrassment especially if your track record with money and credit history isn't a good one. But honesty from the start is very important because you cannot go into a relationship with financial skeletons. Those bones will soon be exposed if you try to buy a car, home, or even trying to rent an apartment.

Most anything you wish to obtain your credit history is attached to you getting it. Or not. When to have "the talk" about money is just as important as the subject itself. During a heated argument is NOT a good time to talk about money. You want to experience some serious mud slingin'? This would be the time. Money arguments can be some of the most explosive arguments couples can have so when it comes to this topic, you have to pick a time that's comfortable and safe to do so.

The word safe sounds crazy I know, but the reality is

this is a hot button topic for some. So having set times to discuss your finances may help in alleviating some of the stress that come with this discussion. Also, a huge thing to understand here is that as a society, men and women just have different views regarding money. The standards put upon a man regarding money are very high and we women do expect those standards to be met. But, with those standards have to come understanding. If you are a young couple dating and getting into your careers or are in college, you can't expect that your man can give you all these gifts and take on added financial responsibilities when he is growing himself.

Paying for all the dinners, dates, movies, birthdays, holidays, night's out. All that adds up! In these modern times, especially young and starting out you have to compromise and co spend. Meaning tonight I got this. Next time, you got it. You have to share the fun of extracurricular expenses.

Now on the flip side of that, growing up my stepfather taught me early. "Shan, if a man asks to take you out, you never go in your pocket. He is asking you so he's gotta pay!" I grew up with that instilled in me and I'll be honest, to this day I still keep to this "covenant." I have honestly never paid for a date. Ok, wait. Yes, I did and to be real with you, it bothered the hell out of me. It was a first date and I wanted to see if as a man if he was comfortable with me paying and he was. So much so that the two other times we went to dinner he didn't ask to contribute. He allowed me to pick up the check every time.

Now in today's modern world, maybe that's ok? I'm not sure. But, all I could think about was that he was comfortable with me going in my pocket three different occasions and said nothing. Truthfully, it bothered me and I could never quite get over that. He was such a nice person, but that always stuck with me and I'll tell you why. I viewed it as selfish. In my opinion he had the opportunity to say, "No let me get it this time" but he didn't.

Needless to say, I walked away from that situation feeling I made the right decision because from what I viewed from the start it just wasn't right for me. I know that for myself as a woman, I do have ideals about men and money and if it doesn't coincide with what feels right to me, I'll either voice my opinion or just walk away. Again, my ideal was what my stepfather instilled in me from a child. Men have to pay.

Now, I am smart enough and considerate enough to know at my level of maturity that there is nothing wrong with me going in my pocket on occasion. Though to be honest and I'm smiling while writing this, the men I've dated and ultimately married, would never be comfortable with that. For the majority, I've been with men, who were raised as I was and were uncomfortable with me picking up the check. Again, it's important to find a compromise and idealistic views with whom you choose to date or marry. Once you're married or living together, by now you both should have a clear view of each other's attitude and understanding of money and managing finances.

I'm telling you now if one of you is secretive or feeling the need to keep up with what others have you are headed for trouble. Let's begin by discussing "secrets." When I say secrets, you do have a clear understanding of what I mean, right? Let's put out some examples if you're unsure. Helping family members with money on a consistent basis or having a shopping addiction. One parent is constantly giving money to their children without discussing it with the other. Loaning money to needy friends because you want to be helpful.

The problem here is that when you begin to make financial decisions that may ultimately affect your home and relationship without discussing it together it creates a shit storm of issues. I personally have been through a few of these examples myself and it put a heavy strain on my relationship at times. Helping out family and friends is fine, but for it to become a strain on one person by keeping it a secret so your partner doesn't get upset is horrible.

Family and friends walk a very fine line in our commitment in wanting to help. Also, they can't always assume you have it because you're always giving it. You cannot put yourselves under that kind of pressure of having to figure out other people's financial situations. Another huge culprit here is children. Real quickly I want to share this. As the adults in the home, we consistently are the example on so many levels. How we communicate, love and respect each other. We also have to realize how we handle and deal with financial matters in our homes, our children view us as an example as well. We have to teach our children at a very early age the importance of saving, having good credit and being fiscally responsible. They have to live the example that this is how you behave with money and your credit.

We've all seen those families that have been on public assistance for generations and we have also seen the opposite of that with families whose children become financially sound as well. It's all in what we teach them and show them consistently.

Now, the subject of children and money can be very touchy for some. I'm very old school. My parent's made us earn our allowance through chores and good grades. You didn't just receive things because they had it or because we wanted it. You had to earn it and some had to go in our piggy banks. My parents didn't buy their children and I raised my child the same way. But, there are many couples on the opposite side of the fence that feel like I do and then there are the ones that buy their children everything to keep them happy or "guilt free" so to speak. Meaning, because you're not always around due to work or career, you feel the need to buy them want they want.

Big thing here, Children need your PRESENCE NOT YOUR PRESENTS! When it comes to your children and money, you have to be on the same page. One child can't go to one parent and get a different answer from the other. WE have to be on the same page. Growing up, if either of my parents found out you went behind their back after you were given a no, your ass is getting whipped. That's just the way it was. You can't have one of you sneaking, buying and giving to keep your kids happy.

Children learn very early the art of manipulation and having them know your weaknesses and varying views on issues like these, they will do what they have to do to get their way. It causes so many arguments and derision. Children have to learn at an early age that they are not in control and that they have to be respectful of both parents at all times. You don't get what you want when you want. Giving into all their wants and demands sets them up to be adults with materialism and arrogance.

Which leads me into my next question. How many of you are "Keeping Up?" Meaning, constantly comparing and needing to have and acquire possessions because this one may or may not have it. The amount of frontin' that people do today has landed so many couples in desperate and financial ruin that it's beyond comprehension. Clearly we have all heard of the phrase "Keeping up with the Jones." But, in doing my interviews so many men shared it was hard for them to keep up with all the materialism.

The pressure of the bags, shoes, clothes, and jewelry is excessive and at times overwhelming. Now, as a woman, in our defense I will say that not ALL women put their men under this kind of pressure. But for all of us that don't, there are many that do. If you take a look at the culture of society today, everything is based on labels and excess. For some women, the need to possess certain "accoutrements" is everything to them and so many men feel to keep this type of woman happy he has to be providing all these things. Keeping up appearances is a real issue for some men and quite honestly it's not something many will openly admit.

Ideally most men want to be able to afford what their women want or need. As I mentioned previously, a man's ego and pride are greatly attached to their ability to earn and contribute. But as a man you also have to look at yourself and question your relationship with this type of woman. Maybe she wasn't always this way, or maybe in the beginning it didn't seem like a problem. But at some point you have to communicate what you will and will not be able to do.

Your ability to "keep up" so to speak will only last so long. Over time, this can cause real resentment. When you start feeling like an ATM and less like a man that's being loved and cared for, eventually, you will get turned off and quite possibly turned on by another woman who sees YOU and not just what you can buy for her. I've always felt that people with the need to want and acquire so excessively have issues that are far deeper than the actual possession. Meaning it's not really about the "red bottom" per say, but more about some form of insecurity and that possession fills a void. Something somewhere is missing in an individual that they feel the need to behave in this way.

Again, when we marry or move in with the person we love it's important to know them for who they truly are. So many situations can be avoided just by paying attention and not turning a blind eye to a red flag, or issue that reared its head to you in the beginning. As my sister Cathy shared with me, and so eloquently I might add, "So many people meet each other, say I love you, move in together, and THEN you start finding out stuff about them! "Oh yeah, I forgot to mention I have two charge offs and we should file separately!" The reality is the money conversation is needed.

Now, from a personal standpoint I was one of those women that in the past, put my complete financial trust in the hands of the person I loved and that is not something I will ever do again. I never questioned or inquired. My lessons were invaluable. We all have to be accountable to ourselves and look out for our best interest financially. What can be difficult for many is to admit that financial hardships have happened and have caused them emotional and financial duress that may affect them for years. It can be a cause of real embarrassment.

But in the interest of love and money, you have to be honest and you have to be upfront about how you're doing financially. As my mom would say, "It's gonna come to light anyway, so you might as well get it over with now!"

On a side note, there were so many sayings that my parents had growing up and as a little girl, I was always like "Ok, I know" but the truth is as an adult woman, they were on point with those one liners! I cannot begin to tell y'all how many times I'm laughing to myself over "getting" it years later.

Ok, back to the marriage of love and money. Ultimately we all want to live well and be with a person that not only truly loves us for who we are but also wants to share in building dreams together. It's important to find someone who has financial goals and dreams similar to your own and equally as important, understanding that these dreams take time, patience and compromise.

If at any point the need to have certain possessions becomes bigger than the relationship then it's time for some real soul searching. Love and money are both necessary. The Real? "Love don't pay bills and money can't buy you love!" But, how great is it that as a couple you can work hard together through mutual understanding and trust in establishing a life that's filled with lots of love and financial security? I openly admit I want both. I not only work hard in establishing myself as an individual, but ultimately one day I hope to meet a man that matches and even exceeds my abilities to have both.

Being able to build together is important because when the success happens it's even sweeter. The struggle, the hard times, the moments of vulnerability will show you how much a person truly loves you. When you have nothing and they're willing to build and sacrifice with you? That trumps any material thing. I've said this to the men I interviewed " If you were to take away all the things that your woman loves, and you could no longer provide those things for her anymore, would your relationship be over?" The answers were not always pleasant needless to say.

Now, again as a woman, I don't want to take on the tone of bashing women. That's not what I want you to take away here. But, what I do want is for people to look at their behaviors and understand how those behaviors impact the people they love. If you're a materialistic person and it's putting a strain on your relationship then you have to sit with that and look that in the face and do something about it. Materialism to me is selfish. It doesn't allow you to see past yourself and hurts the people around you.

Again, as I have stated previously, part of being an adult is recognizing our faults and being proactive in changing them. In loving a man, we accept him. We accept that at this moment, in this time, this is what he can give. If he is not meeting your expectations based upon your criteria, then it's a choice you made, that you have to be accountable for. If your man isn't well off or wealthy, you knew that going in. Placing unrealistic expectations on him will not help your relationship. I always remind my female friends to meet their men we're that at, especially financially.

If he's in school, in a trade, or building his career he needs time to get up and running and established. You have to be patient in that way. You have to be understanding. Things will come. Careers, friends, and even family can all put us in the position of wanting to keep up and be a part of something greater. There is absolutely nothing wrong with wanting to obtain. The fine line of what's more important is what has to be understood here.

What I've learned over time with this whole "Keeping up with the Jones" thing is that it's not really about what they have. More importantly. it's more about what you see in them that you wish you had. Maybe their drive, or love for each other? They appear to you to have it all. Most times, as we all suspect, things are never what they seem. The Jones's, in all actuality, may wish to have what you have which may go beyond any materialism.

I don't know how many women I know that appear to have it all but are miserable inside and at home. The love doesn't equal the money or you're paying a high price for the possession. Whatever it is, allow the communication to flow in an honest way and be kind to each other. Think of how impactful the word "kind" is and what that can do for your relationships or marriages.

With kindness comes understanding. Marrying love and money is a beautiful thing to me. Being able to provide well for your families and each other is gratifying to say the least. Never allow someone else's standards to dictate or get in the way of your love and respect for each other. Communicate, be honest, be realistic and most importantly be understanding in building your "Benjamin's" together!

CHAPTER 4
LET'S GET IT ON!!

"Having sex is like playing bridge. If you don't have a good partner, you'd better have a good hand!"
- Woody Allen

Warning! This chapter contains explicit material that may be offensive to some. Reader discretion is advised! I'm a naughty girl. Wait, let me rephrase that, I'm a VERY NAUGHTY GIRL!! I absolutely, positively, and resolutely love SEX! I openly admit to being a very passionate, lustful and sensual woman. Sex and intimacy are by far my favorite topics to talk about.

With that being said, I'm going to reiterate to you that I'm going to speak very candidly and explicitly so if you find yourself clutching your pearls or sweating, don't say I didn't warn you! Sex. To me, it's the ultimate form of self-expression. As a sexually confident woman, I fully embrace the power it gives me. Men are extremely turned on by that power. There is nothing more seductive and attractive to a man than a woman who is confident in herself and her ability to give pleasure with no hang ups or insecurities.

A woman who carries herself with such assurance that he knows when they enter that bedroom he can be his ultimate sexual self. Allowing him to take as much as he wants and giving him everything he asks for. He doesn't have to say anything because their chemistry allows her to know everything.

She is confident in what she gives and expects him to beg for more. Yes ladies, men love that shit! The art of making love and fucking, yes they are two different forms of expression, is one of the most powerful gifts we have. I say it's a gift because not everyone is good at it. I happen to be great at it. I know it and I'm proud of it. It's a "gift" that I've shared with a select few and let's just say I have left a formidable memory! Now, what you're probably thinking is, "Shanda, what makes your gift so memorable?" Well, as a woman I've learned the value of being in tuned to a man sexually. I listen, I take direction and I also give direction. I'm not quick to say no because I'm extremely enthusiastic regarding sex and intimacy. Actually, my problem is I never say no!

I'm laughing while writing this!! My birthday is 6/9 so I'm thinking this sex drive was in the stars for me?! But, getting back to the sex, I just love it! I'm sexually confident in the way that I kiss, lick, suck, fuck and make love to a man. All those things a man needs in his woman. Ladies, if you are lacking in enthusiasm and confidence it's going to strain your sexual relationship. You have to be aware of your power and use it! Your man should never be asking for it.

I demand my intimacy. I have expectations that need to be met. I will share with you at the very beginning of my relationships, when the sex talk happens I'm very honest about my high sex drive. I've found that most men find it a turn on. Initially. Though, in the relationship, they look at me, like "Damn you wasn't joking about that shit!!" Yes, I'm known to live up to my proclamation! But, I'm also sensitive enough to know that at times those demands can't always be met. In either case, the importance of understanding and knowing your partner is essential in pleasing each other.

Firstly, you have to have your "mental" in order for sex to be great for either one of you. The largest sexual organ we possess is our brain. If there is a block or hang up regarding sex and intimacy, it can sabotage your ability to let go and give and receive pleasure. Before, I get to what I like to call the "good stuff" let's discuss some hang ups that impede us women.

For many of us, one of the first things we do is turn the lights off. We women can get very nervous about them bright lights being on. We are not always fully confident in how our bodies look and though we may see our faults, most men do not. "Oh, my stomach is too big, I hate my stretch marks, I have cellulite!" Hey ladies, even with all those concerns, they still want them lights on and want to see everything!

I have NEVER in my life been with a man that complained of his thighs or his stomach being too big. They for the most part present dick and all like, "What's up! Let's do this!" I love and admire that so much. They don't get all crazy like we women can. Believe me ladies, they already can tell the package by how it's wrapped. They know what it is. Spanx or not. They want to see it all, up close and personal. But, if the lights are still too uncomfortable for you, a great compromise, which I love, is either a dimmer on your lamps or candles.

I'm all about all the senses being engaged, so I really love scented candles. Scented candles and dick? What?!! Love it!! Also music. It can help in soothing you and letting down your inhibitions as well. Believe me, between the candles and soft music, them legs will open wide like the great divide! The beauty of the candles too is the shadow they create on your walls and ceiling. Don't believe me? Just watch!!

Another concern many women have honestly is smell and discharge. This is not something women openly admit to and find extremely uncomfortable to talk about, but for so many not having what I call, "vaginal confidence" is a real concern. Here's the thing, the vagina has to be well taken care of. That bad boy has to be healthy and smelling right. If not, it can ruin your confidence and your partner may never wish to partake from it again.

Many women feel more comfortable showering or bathing prior to sex. They want to smell and feel "fresh" down there. Though, be careful using sprays, wipes and powders. And ladies, real quick, let's relax with the powder! Your bottom should not be emitting powder puffs because you OD'd on the talc! Whatever your vaginal concerns are and without going too deep into this subject, discuss with your physician your options. Either way, whatever remedies they suggest that are healthiest for you should help in relieving your anxieties some.

Other issues like vaginal dryness and lack of sex drive should also be discussed with your doctor as well. Again, as I've stated before, whatever concerns we have regarding our lives, we have to address them. We have to be proactive even with our sexual health. What we don't take care of and what we allow to fester not only affects us, but greatly affects our partners and our ability to have a healthy relationship or marriage. We have to clear our minds before our bodies can have full enjoyment. With that being said, let's get to the good stuff!!

Now, before I dive in, I want to state clearly, everything I say and suggest is based on you knowing not only your HIV and STD status but your partner's as well. I love sex without reservation, so in order for any of us to have that, we have to be assured in knowing "it's all good" for us to get down. So, let's have some fun!

Question. What turns you on? While you're reading

this, I want you to really contemplate that, then ask yourself if your man or your woman knows what TRULY turns you on. Are you getting what you want and desire sexually? Now, I'm going to be honest and share with you that as a woman, I truly love having what I call "quality control" talks with my man. You know how when you're on one of those business calls and they say, "This call may be monitored for quality control purposes. To better assist our customers for future service."

See, these talks allow me to keep my game up so to speak in pleasing him. I NEVER take anything for granted sexually so I like to always ask consistently what he would like or is there something I'm doing that he doesn't like. Now, I never get any complaints. I just like assuring him that I cater to him sexually. It also keeps me fulfilled as well because it allows constant communication to flow between us. As I stated earlier in this chapter, I'm a very naughty girl. I love sex that allows me to be free spirited. I'm very big on a man dominating me sexually.

I have a strong personality, so I love a man that handles me in a way that he's my boss. It's a huge turn on for me not only physically but mentally as well. I saw a movie years ago with David Spade and Maggie Gyllenhaal named The Secretary and it had me open! If you've never watched it, after reading this chapter I'm sure you will! But, it's all about him telling her what to do and ordering her around. I love that! The spanking and hair pulling! I also love in the middle of sex when a man is telling me, what I'm gonna do! "You gonna go cook me something to eat! You gonna run me a bath! Then you gonna take your ass to sleep after I'm done fuckin' you! You hear me?!!!" Yes, Daddy!! All of this is being whispered in my ear while he's spanking me and hitting it from the back! What?!! I'm getting hot just writing this!

Now, as quick as I am to take direction, I also enjoy giving direction! One of my favorite sexual past times is to jerk my man off. I love giving head to, which will get its own chapter, but there's something very special and dominant in jerking a man off. I want you to close your eyes and imagine this scenario.

It's been a long day. You and your man are in bed relaxing. You've both had your showers and it's pillow talk time. You know he wants some, but tonight you're a little tired and not up for sex as much as he is. You're talking and rubbing his chest. You see his manhood rising beneath the covers. Now, he would love more than anything for you to blow him right now. And you can mention that to him. You say " Bae, you want some don't you?" chuckling softly. He gives you that low "yeah" with that look in his eye and that little thrust they give. "Mommy's got you." Now, you're not really up for head either. There are just days we don't wish to give it, and that's cool, but you still want to please him.

Here is where your hands do all the work. Now, this act is all about control and visualization. One thing I want to express to you ladies, men are very visual beings. In having great sex, they love watching you in every aspect. This particular hand job act is no exception. So, let him lay back and relax. By now you should have a clear idea of how much lube he likes. Some men prefer more, some less. Have him spread his legs wide. Take your top off slowly in front of him. Believe me he wants to see them titties. Now, personally I like to keep my bra on at the start. A nice sexy bra, while you're jerking him is a great visualization.

Now, let's start jerking! Start slowly at first. Some long and deep strokes. Just very lightly. Allow his reaction to give you direction. His breathing and his moaning will clearly tell you how well your rhythm is. This is the time, when I love to start talking. Ask him how much he likes it. Does it feel good? Bend forward towards his dick almost like you're going to suck it. Make him think you are. He's going to get excited even more. Work your hand real good and keep talking to him. Take his hand and put it on your breast. If your bra is on he's going to pull one of them titties out at this time. He's gonna start working your nipple also.

Now, if he's doing that, it's going to get you going as well, which will only increase your hand action. Again, by his reaction, you can tell if he's ready to cum. If he is, tell him you're not ready for him to cum, and stop. Now, you have to be real careful ladies at this point because you don't want to get him so close to the edge that he cum's anyway because he couldn't control it. He's going to beg you to keep going and you tell him no. "You cum when I let you cum!" Now, with him so close, some men may even have a little pre cum visible. If, you're into tasting, slowly with your finger take this and dab it on your tongue. This move right here, will have him very close to exploding, but this is also a good time for you to take your bra off completely and let him watch you. Make him ask for you to take him back in your hand. When you do, start at the head and continue until he can't take it anymore. Instruct him to tell you when he's ready cum! When he's close and you can tell by his breathing and reaction, use your other hand to play with his nuts.

By now he may have both your titties in his hands! Just before he's ready to blow, to give him that ultimate orgasm, ask him this, "Baby you wanna cum in my face, my mouth or on my titties?" Just you asking him will probably have him over the edge by now!! Work him over until he's cumming all over the place. Now, personally if it's on my face or on my breasts, I'll moan too and I'll rub it in my titties in front of him. He more than likely will say " You so nasty" in a good way! Then it's clean up with the warm rag time. Wipe him off, let him air dry, then put him to bed. With a smile. Everybody's happy and can go to sleep like babies! Don't you just love storytime?

Now, let's talk fucking. As I mentioned earlier, in my opinion fucking and love making are two different forms of expression. Fucking is that animalistic, carnal, hot and heavy expression. It allows you to be nasty and dirty. When I use those words, I mean in it in the context of allowing the freak in you to dominate.

For me, I love fucking outside. My ex and I use to do it all the time and it was some of the most memorable moments of my life! In the rain, outside bent over just having a good ole time! It's all about letting go and being free of judgement and scrutiny. You allow yourself to take and give in the most explicit manner. What is "fucking" to you? Have you been allowed to let yourself go in the most completely rapacious way? For many women even having these kinds of discussions may feel very unladylike.

What I'd like to share and what I want every woman reading this to understand is that allowing yourself this form of expression is freedom. It doesn't' make you any less a lady if it's done with your man or your husband. Even as a single woman, if you handle your business in a way that's private, mature and responsible, let go without reservation.

We women are very aware of the how society views us and how we are expected to behave. There is a double standard in regards to sex and men and women. Men are considered a stud when he conquers and fucks and we women are often looked upon as hoes. Plain and simple. I honestly don't buy into it at all.

As adults, we all should embrace our sexuality with honesty and responsibility in a way that empowers us. For me, fucking is a form of expression that allows me to tap into that wild woman inside of me. I love her! She gets spanked, talks dirty and her hair pulled!! Oh, let's talk hair real quick. Now, in this modern day of wigs and weaves, the reality is men are going to try to touch your hair in some way. This is a real concern for some women because the last thing they want is a man all up in they tracks. Men for the most part don't mind weaves that look believable and that are well done. If it's looking like a hot mess, it can be a real turn off. When you're giving head, or bent over doggy style, 9 times out of 10 your hair is getting touched. Unless, you tell him off limits! Some ladies will let him know, "Don't touch my hair!" But, for the ones that don't just make sure your weave is secure and sewn in well.

The reality is most men are "Hair Weave Killas!" They gonna sweat your joint out and have you lookin' like a crazy woman with your hair all over the place! I don't know how many times, I personally have looked in the mirror and said to myself, "You LOOK like you been fuckin'!" It's true! We look a hot mess sometimes, but it's so worth it! Them "jam sessions" can get real intense and have us swinging from the chandeliers! I also love the residual symptoms of fuckin'. The next day, when you're at work or even in the car driving and your mind replays what happened the night before and you get that little chill down your back? It's like "Whoa" You start smiling and laughing to yourself about how naughty yall behaved. Going over scenarios about the next time and how this part was really good.

Look, my mind stays in the sex clouds as it is, so replaying it in my mind is another high for me as well. It gets me hyped for the next encounter. I also love thinking about trying something new that I'll throw into the mix to keep his mind and body guessing. I don't like predictability and trust me ladies, men don't either. In numerous interviews what was shared was that men for the most part love for their woman to be unpredictable. Loves for her to do something so unexpected and fun that he had no idea she had it in her. They don't want to have to know her every move. They love when a woman is proactive. Here's a little thing I want you ladies to try. Let's say it's a Thursday evening. Your family has already had dinner. Homework is done. The kids are in the living room watching their cartoons. Your man is in his office or the basement working on whatever. You take a quick scan. Everything for the most part is pretty quiet. This is when you call out to your man and say, "Babe, can you come here for a minute I need to show you something." Now, he may be on a call or on the computer and you may have to call him two or three times. "Babe, please it's really important!" He will more than likely yell, "Ok, I'm coming now." Now, you're in the bathroom. He's gonna go looking for you in the bedroom. You say, "Babe, I'm in here. I have to show you this!" Now, the fact that you're in the bathroom he's going to assume that some sort of female problem is going on and he's gonna roll his eyes up in the back of his head and probably be thinking "Here we go." He enters the bathroom and you ask him to close the door. By now he is thinking what in the hell is wrong?? This is when you say "Baby, nothing's wrong, I just wanna suck your dick!"

You pull him to you, kiss him, and take his Johnson out his pants. You put the toilet seat down, sit there and handle your business. By this time, the kids are being nosy because things are too quiet and 9 times out of 10 in the middle of daddy getting serviced your man will holler to the kids, that y'all will be downstairs in a minute. See, it's those little unexpected moments of intimacy and naughtiness that men love. And ladies, all of what I've shared is not to negate our needs. We want the same care and attention. But, as a woman don't be afraid to take the reins and do things that are fun and out of the ordinary that keep your sex life fresh and exciting. It truly benefits the both of you!

Now, how many of you like to play with "toys?" I do! Yeah, buddy!! The Rabbit, The Bullet, The Tongue. Those names sound familiar? If you're a "toy enthusiast" like myself, you know those names are as popular as Mickey D's! Bringing these into your bedroom with your man is definitely a fun way of taking your sex lives to another level. Men for the most part don't mind them, but for some they don't care for them at all. Now, here fellas, is where I don't get it. If you're one of those dudes that's not into it, I get that you have your preference. But, what I will say is if it pleases your woman, why not compromise on the type of toy being used? Maybe some men feel less than compared to "Big Black" or "Great White" in your drawer? I don't know.

Whatever the concern, I do believe there is a common ground in between. For you gentleman that say no way, or are a bit of a control freak sexually, imagine this scene. It's going down. You and your woman are hot and heavy. But, tonight she decides to go in a different direction. Don't complain, don't question. Just watch. She asks you to take a seat at the edge of the bed. You watch her take baby oil and shine up her body very slowly and sensually for you.

You're not allowed to touch her. Yet. But, you are allowed to stroke your dick while you're watching her. As she is shining her body down she spreads her legs wide and begins to shine her pussy for you. Spreading herself wide and exposing her clit for you. You watch while she caresses her nipples with one hand and rubbing her clit with the other. Her body is primed and by now you're ready to see her orgasm spill across her face. But, unexpectedly she pulls out her surprise! The Bullet! She places it on her clit and begins to squirm and moan your name softly then loudly. She asks you to come to her. She instructs you to finger her while the bullet is stimulating her clit. Listen and do as you're told! Now gentleman, you get the picture? I hope so!

Allowing some "additions" other than your "wanker" should not always come with a no. But more of a let's "see" what happens! Don't be afraid to let go of some control guys. Think of how good it feels that you can sit back and put your hands behind your neck and just be taken advantage of and given some direction. Sex is like a diamond. You know how a diamond should have the highest ratings with the 4 C'S? Sex's 4C's are Communication, Compromise, Commitment and Contentment. You both have to prioritize this part of your relationship more than most areas because within the boundaries of monogamy all you have is each other. Being accountable to those 4 C's means you're important to each other and that you value each other sexually and intimately. It's not something your friends, family, kids anyone else shares in. It's you two, so it has to be handled with lots of care and attention.

Sex is a powerful drug and when it is fed properly it allows relationships and marriages to flourish. It's a component that cannot be replaced and should always be updated! Keep things fresh and new. Wear sexy clothing. Surprise him with some lingerie. Some men even love the simplicity of a t-shirt or boy shorts. Whatever turns him on, do it. Whatever turns her on, do it. You both should be fully aware of each other's turn-ons and erogenous zones. The neck kiss and soft whisper in my ear drives me crazy!! Even touching me on my arm lightly will take me over the edge with a man. The key is in KNOWING what your partner likes. Likes are very important.

Men like a lot of things sexually. A very big "like" they love is anal sex. Now, ladies, I'm going to tread real lightly on this subject. Many of you are dead against it. And, I get it. It can be extremely painful and hurtful if done improperly. Anal sex can be a highly pleasurable experience if you're both into it. One can't be in and the other out. Because it is a highly mental, emotional and physical act, it has to be handled very delicately. If your woman is not used to it or never tried it, you have to go at her pace.

Honestly some women have experienced it and will never do it again. If that is the case, you have to understand that. You can't make her do it. But, if she is open to experimenting then you both should have an understanding about how it's done. Of course, this form of sex is highly recognized by some as taboo. A huge percentage of women feel that area is strictly an exit not an enter. Though there are some of us women, myself included that indulge in it and find it very pleasurable. The key is stimulating the mind, the area, lubing it properly, and going at a pace that is pleasurable for both of you. Again, it's all about the communication.

As a couple, there will be things that both of you will say yes and no to. Let me share another big "like" men have. Porn. Now, again, I'm waving the flag for porn as well! Y'all probably thinking, "Damn, Shanda, what don't you like?!" but I do love it! I believe it can add real excitement to your relationship or marriage. Now, many women, no matter how much I advocate porn are just not into it. And that's fine, but don't be crazy if your man is.

Men love looking at ass, titties, blowjobs, and two women getting it on. Is it nasty? Maybe. I say this with a smile by the way, but, they love their quiet moments looking at all sorts of sex. Given the quiet opportunity they will be jerking off and masturbating as well. It's healthy. The problems begin when we as women judge them for this. Now, I want to be clear in saying that I do believe that a man watching and indulging in porn is fine. But, when it becomes excessive and interferes with your sex life or he feels he cannot function without it, then that's a problem. And it's definitely not one I can solve in this book, so an appointment with a sex therapist may be what needs to happen. But, men love voyeurism and I think even incorporating into your sex can be highly enjoyable.

Listen, try this. Have your man pick what movie he loves. Believe me ladies, he has his favorites. Let him watch it hands free while you're blowing him. Or put on a movie you find pleasurable and let him lick you while you're watching. Now a days, couples are going to strip clubs together. They both are making it rain! Ultimately what I would like to stress is do what makes you EQUALLY happy. What works for one couple may not work for another.

With that being said, I want to also share that when it comes to your sex lives, keep it private. There are certain friendships that we women and men have that we trust in discussing our intimacy with. Certain areas of your life, I believe should be kept special just between the two of you. You have to understand that with certain information you're inviting others into the bedroom with you. Which in turn allows others to make comments, criticisms and assessments. That's not always cool to do.

Your sex lives should be shared, if ever with people you trust implicitly. Which leads me into ménage a trois. Sigh. I'm going to be very clear on my opinion with the threesome issue. As a single person, if this is something you wish to partake in, and you're practicing safe sex, go ahead. YOLO. But, when you are in a monogamous relationship and you start asking your partner to live out your fantasy because you would oh so love it, you have to be prepared for a no. Or if it is done, be prepared for the possible consequences of this action and what it can do to your relationship.

I am one of the most open minded people I know, but I have witnessed too many negative affects regarding this topic. As a woman, I'm very aware that many men would love this experience. I get it. I have female friends that have enjoyed it as well. But, when it comes to committed relationships and marriages, I truly believe it's something you need to do prior to monogamy. Inviting "guests" into your bedroom can bring a host of issues that you were not prepared for.

Now, if it's an agreed upon understanding and you both enjoy it. Go for it. For me, I'm the only bitch in the room, so Shanda ain't having no extras unless it's them toys I spoke about! But, getting back to the subject of privacy, there may be occasions you need that outlet of trust to discuss certain things. Or even advice. Just be mindful of whom you share that delicate information with. Once it's out there it can't be taken back.

In moving forward positively in this great subject of sex and intimacy, remember to have fun! Text each other, always be aware of your partner's needs and communicate.

When it comes to positions, switch it up! Take it outside, in the car! In the laundry room!! Be spontaneous! Make shit exciting!

When things get stagnant and you become unhappy you have to speak up. And when you do put it in a way that doesn't strip your partner of their dignity. Always be mindful of their feelings. Handle them with kid gloves. Maligning a person about their sexuality is painful, so you have to be very cognizant of their feelings. But, even more so, empower each other sexually. Complaints can easily spill out of our mouths, but kindness and generosity fuels not only our egos but our relationships. Also as a woman, don't censor yourself. Don't be afraid to let go and embrace your sexual self.

Men love that and are drawn to that confidence. They want to hear what pleases you! Give him direction and guidance. Believe me they don't mind being the student if they trust their teacher! Fellas, give as much as you receive! Don't just be a taker. Feed your woman's emotional needs with the balance of her physical desires. Let her know how good she tastes and how great her head game is! Most importantly, show how much you love her. Be supportive of each other sexually and emotionally. Don't let comfortability turn your bedroom into a "bored room!" Be each other's cheerleaders!!! Because when it comes to the game of sex and your partner, remember "There is no I in TEAM!!!.

CHAPTER 5
HEAD GAMES

"Clinton lied. A man might forget where he parks or where he lives, but he never forgets oral sex, no matter how bad it is." – Barbara Bush

Babs was on the money with that quote! One thing a man won't forget is head! Good or bad!

Fellatio. It shines bright like a diamond in its hierarchy of sexual fulfillment! So much so, I had to give it its own chapter. MEN LOVE HEAD!! You wanna keep your man happy? Make sure your head game is on point! You gotta slob on that knob ladies! I know that sounds graphic, but it's important that I get your attention here! Your mouth and the power it holds conveys more than mere words love.

The ability to perform great head is a huge asset. Yes, ladies it's an asset. Sharing your mouth is as important to your man as sharing your body. For some men, maybe even more so. His cup needth to runneth over with your head game!

So what makes a good "HEADSTRESS?" For one, ENTHUSIASM!!! There is nothing more gratifying to a man than watching a woman who's thoroughly enjoying sucking, licking and yes even swallowing him. "I been drankin, I been drankin!" I had to throw that in there! You have to suck his penis like you want to draw diamonds out of it! Think of how hard you gonna go at sucking it if he was actually spurting diamonds girls?!! Exactly! You cannot act like you'd rather be playing Scrabble than sucking his penis. That's a no no ladies. He honestly would rather just zip his pants up and walk away. Him and his bottom lip. Truthfully, I love the power that giving great head allows me. That very confidence empowers me. I feel like Wonder Woman when I'm performing it because I know, not only am I enjoying myself giving it but I'm turned on even more so of how my skills affect him.

I love watching a man with his head back, eyes rolled to the back of his head, biting his bottom lip. Saying, "dam babe! That shit feels so good!" Holding the back of your neck while your mouth is sliding up and down all over his manhood. He wants to watch all that. He wants to see and hear how good he tastes to you.

You have to be very explicit when you are sucking him. Don't be shy and hold back because this is the time that he NEEDS to hear how nasty you can be. Allow him to give you direction. If he wants you to concentrate more on the head, then suck that bad boy like a Blow Pop. Pun intended! If he wants you to suck it with long strokes then do that. Make him spread his legs wide for you. Kneel down slowly in front of him with your heels on and commence to sucking him like your life depends on it! When you take command of that power in giving your man that fulfillment, that right there will keep his ass happy! Allowing him the freedom of brains on demand is another novelty some men wish they had as well.

I have interviewed countless men who wish they could

have "head without a headache." Listen, I know this chapter is challenging to many of you women who are not "head enthusiasts." But, the reality is that the majority of men crave the warmth and wetness of your mouth. And ladies, do not get it twisted. Even if your nooky is blooming flowers and emits sweet honey, it does not replace good head! Now, I have come across some men who are not all that into receiving head, but they were far and few between. As a whole, the majority of men love it and want it on a consistent basis. They want you to tap into the "nasty girl" inside of you and please him in the most erotic ways possible. "Sloppy top" is a favorite with so many men because of its very connotation. Sucking him in a way almost like you're slurping it. Extra wet and extra noisy. Deep throating him while your hand is jerking him as well. All of this lends to a man's senses. Visually it takes him over the top and again, your enthusiasm and drive in pleasing him with your mouth is everything to him!

Honestly a man can lose major interest in you if you're not one to please him orally. And believe me, I have heard many women complain that they just don't like it. But, if your man loves it, and he's giving you good head then you have to figure out a compromise. Now some men have penis's that are just too big. All of us ladies have at some point dealt with a man whose Johnson made you wish you had elastic on the side of your mouth! Those bad boys are work! You gotta put in toil with the big dogs! If this is an "issue" for you then honestly you have to give him the "one two!" Meaning you suck as far down as you can and let your hand do the rest. If it's just the head, then that's all he can get. But let your hands and your willingness to please him handle the rest.

On the flip side, we also have at some point dealt with the smaller ones as well. If he has a smaller penis, honestly you should be handling him like bubble gum! You should be chomping away, blowing bubbles and errrrythang! The smaller ones are light work. And I don't mean that in a defamatory way. I mean it in the way that it's much more comfortable to fit it in your mouth with no issue.

It's funny to me how men with very large penis's think it's the bees knees. But the reality is too much dick can be painful and can cause a problem in you wanting to have sex and give head for some women. A man can't make his penis smaller, so if you have a "big man" you have to be able to take him on so he can be happy.

Giving good head has necessary components. Let's start at the beginning! As stated earlier, Enthusiasm. You have to let him know this is something you enjoy doing, better yet, in your mind I want you to think like you're gonna take him down! Make his knees buckle!

Secondly, you want to start with a warm mouth ladies. Have a few sips of warm water if you had something cold to drink prior to you giving him head. I share this little tip with you because men with their penises hate the cold. They instantly shrivel up. It's like when a man dives into a pool of cold water. Them nuts shrivel right up! You want your mouth to feel like warm apple pie! A man's penis craves a warm and wet opening so when you are performing oral sex on him keep that in mind.

Next, technique is EVERYTHING!! Your flow and how you handle him comes with practice. It's like riding a bike. You gotta get on and keep practicing. For the most part, go by his direction. Encourage him to be vocal. During your sucking noises, you should be asking him how it feels, how he likes it. Even better, if he loves it! Also, do not forget his balls ladies. I know, they ain't the prettiest things to look at, but have fun with them. Men love when you hold them and lightly suck and pull on them. You should be doing this while alternatively sucking him.

Another good move. Hold his nuts taut. Not too tight, you don't want him yelping out in pain. But just enough. His penis will get stiffer and stand up even straighter. When it's like this, you should be able to suck him even better now! Men I've found love that move! He's getting the stimulation on his sack as well as your mouth all over him. Another hot move ladies is to not let him get too use to your rhythm. Try this. Suck just the tip for a sec. Then go down a little further just past the tip. Do that enough that you think he's use to this rhythm. Out of nowhere, take it all the way down to the shaft. Almost to the point of gagging. Not completely now.

Side note, I can't encourage the gagging thing fellas. It gives the sensation of wanting to vomit if it goes down too far. I'm sorry, but it does. Deep throat? Yay! But the gagging thing? Come on with that?! Ok, so getting back to sucking him. Throw in a few surprises like rubbing his nipples with your free hand while you're sucking him. A majority of men love getting their nipples sucked and pulled on so if you know this is something he loves you can incorporate it into this.

Real quick, and I cannot move forward here without mentioning teeth. You gotta watch your teeth ladies. Men don't want you chomping on them with all your porcelain. Have at him with gusto just don't let your overzealousness get your teeth involved ok? Now, another great thing about head is that you're completely in control. Just like the hand jobs, allow yourself to take control of him and to direct him as well. Believe me when I tell you, his ass will listen!

Also ladies, keep your shoes on!! Please no Uggs! Unless of course he likes them. But something really sexy. Some men even love just a thigh high sock or stockings as well! Remember he's visual so it all ties in. So now with all this great sucking that you're doing, your man is ready to cum. Here's where it gets interesting. And here's where I discuss swallowing. Now ladies, don't turn red on me here. After the last chapter and this one, you had to know that I was going to land here.

Swallowing. To swallow or not to swallow? That is the question. Welp. If I tell you to let him ejaculate in your mouth, you may say hell naw! Or, you may be down with it. What I will say and not that it's a big surprise, they love to see you take their sperm in your mouth. Plain and simple. You have to understand that when a man is ejaculating, he is experiencing his waves of orgasm. When you are sucking him and then you stop when he is ejaculating, it cuts back on his intensity. When you allow him to ejaculate in your mouth, you allow him a mind blowing orgasm because there is no cessation. The cherry on the top as well again, visually they love watching this. Now, some women are down with this. But, they ain't gonna swallow it. What I suggest is if you're going to let him ejaculate in your mouth, but you're not going to swallow it, have a towel nearby or something you can spit into. Just do it kind of discreetly.

There's nothing worse than you giving great head then you spoiling it at the end spitting into a towel and saying "yuck" at the end of it all. Just spit and smile ladies. Spit and smile.

Now, for you ride or die sisters you just take it down straight no chaser! Well, maybe some orange juice or apple juice. To quench it down a little. Either way, men love the fact that we've showed up, performed and brought the house down! And fellas, remember what you eat plays into how your sperm tastes. Be aware if you're a smoker and eating certain foods can negatively affect the taste of sperm. Lots of fruit is good. How do I know this? Well, a very good "friend" told me!

Anyway, I'm all for you guys getting your head game on a regular. The reason I'm such a strong advocate is because I believe in getting what I'm giving. So, with all the love I've showered on you gentleman, you best believe your ladies expect you to return the favor. I cannot advocate us women giving and giving without receiving.

We ladies want you to go down on us too. We don't want to hear about no cultural hang ups or any other issues. Unless of course they're valid. But guys you can't be selfish. It's all about reciprocity loves! 69 was a good year!

Yall know what I'm talking bout! Talk about a position that is generous?! We both give and we both receive! At the same damn time!! I'm going to honestly share what I love about this position. For one, the dick is just right there. Up close and personal. If you're sitting on your man's face and your face down on his penis, this allows you to be over it and just sucking it to oblivion.

The beauty of a great suck is how well he's sucking you. Him sucking you ever so lovely will fuel you to suck him even better. Now, sometimes they'll suck it so good, you have to come up off the dick for a second because you're into the sensation of him sucking your clit so well. A man can take you completely over the edge in this position. Just make sure you take him with you! I personally would prefer for us to orgasm simultaneously! That ish right there is beyond beautiful to me!

Whomever orgasms first, the key is that you make each other happy. Ultimately when it comes to sex and intimacy we do what makes us happy and what feels right for us to do. Giving and receiving has to be shared and it has to be a priority. To both of you. One can't feed the fire for both. Not for an extended amount of time. The flame will die out real fast. As far as the head game goes, ladies, treat his penis like it's your best friend. Kiss it. Talk to him. Let him know he is the sweetest thing in the world to you! Tell him you love him! That he's your "Diamonds and Pearls!!"

Pro Man Woman

"I've been married 32 years because my wife and I communicate and respect each other."
                                                    -Domingo Nunez

CHAPTER 6
LOVE IS ALL WE NEED

"Love is composed of a single soul inhabiting two bodies." – Aristotle

Love. The very word itself evokes emotion. The greatest feeling we have the honor of possessing is Love. This four letter word has the ability to make or break the mightiest of men. Men and their hearts. For many of us women, it's the greatest treasure we can possess. There is no jewel or possession on this Earth that can compare to winning the heart of the man we truly love.

How we give love and our ability to receive love is the foundation of every relationship and marriage. Who we decide to love plays a huge part in our ability to have meaningful relationships. I read a quote once that said, "You've got to find people who love like you do." This quote really hit home and it truly was a light bulb moment in affirmation for me. Finding the "like" kind of person to love is the key to great love.

The scales of love are often times unbalanced. We have heard and experienced these very words far too often. Writing this chapter was so profound for me because in looking at my own relationships in regards to the men that I've loved, I realized that how we loved, and how we manifested love was vastly different.

I believe so many of us love a person a certain way, based on what we know love to be. What we experienced as children. How love was represented and expressed before our eyes. All these factors play a huge role in how we are able to give and receive love. What were our parent's example in representing love to us? Did we see and experience them being openly affectionate with each other? Were the words "I love you" said often? How was communication represented? Was it through love and affection or through physical confrontations and yelling?

Growing up in a family of seven my parents raised us to be very affectionate. We were always saying I love you to each other. My mom had this thing where if we were caught fighting, we would both get spankings and then she would make us hug each other and say I love you and then we had to all go to bed.

I watched my parents be openly affectionate with each other without reserve. I realize that in sharing my feelings so openly and consistently my upbringing had a huge impact on me. As a matured woman in sharing my life and story of love with you, I had to dig deep within myself and look at how I love and how I received love. I know that I want to give all of me when I love a man. In looking back in things that I needed to change I had to really reevaluate this point. All of me? What does this mean? Well, it was important for me to give the man I love my good, my great, my mishaps and fully share all my emotions without reserve.

It was always important that I let my man know that I was all in physically, emotionally and mentally. As a young woman, my mother shared with me "Shan, keep some of yourself for yourself. Don't give everything. The wrong person will take it all and leave you with nothing." Of course, this is a lesson that I had to learn through experience. She was right. There are times in our lives when we love with so much conviction, and it's not reciprocated.

It can be a very hurtful place when you love a person so much and give so much of yourself and they don't understand or have the capacity to give you what you need emotionally, mentally and physically in return. This is why it's so very important as individuals from the very beginning to know exactly the kind of love we need that fulfills us and makes us happy. Having a relationship or marriage is saying you're allowing an individual the duty of putting your heart in their hands and that they'll protect it at all costs.

The truth is not everyone is built for that task or they lack certain aspects that you need to be happy in love. For me, there are just certain standards that I need for me to feel like love is flowing between us substantially. As I stated earlier in this chapter, love is an honor. I'm not sure if many of us look at love this way. This word is often times thrown around very freely by some, but if you really look at how important it is for you to love someone it has to feel honorable to you. Associating honor to love means you take it seriously and that you give your word and follow through to it.

Having someone in your life that honors you and your love for each other is crucial. It's like achieving the Medal of Honor in the military. It's the highest form of achievement one can possess. Honor comes with consistency and implementation. Meaning, don't just tell me you love me but show me on a consistent basis in a way that is important to me. Honor me through your actions, communication and emotion.

Honor was such an important piece for me as well because when we fall in love with someone and when we are at a place of being comfortable enough to say it and express it through our actions we have to realize just how important an honor it is that someone loves us the way that we need them to. They chose us to love. That choice if it feels right to you has to be treated with honor and respect because love is not something we should just expect from someone.

So when given by the person we appreciate and love we have to show our respect in their choice in choosing us to love. Respect is another important principle needed in loving a person. How great is the respect that you carry for yourself? Before you can even think about giving another person respect, you have to fully be aware of your own. It puts you in the position of knowing what you deserve and what you will or will not tolerate from another person.

I know when I'm engaging with a man, I watch and pay attention in how he shows respects for himself and others around him. Is he good to people? How does he communicate with others? Does he show humility or arrogance? In observing how he treats his peers and his family, I get a sense of who he is at his core. When it comes to me as a woman, I need a man that respects how he speaks to me, and equally how he treats me. Is he always conscious of my feelings and how his behavior affects me? In loving him, these factors are very important in me giving him love as well. My respect for him is a priority because I value him. Honestly he is a reflection of my choices.

So, in loving a man at this point in my life he has to be a man of substance and caliber. Through my experiences of being in love, he will need to be a man that embodies this aspect of love that is very critical to me.

With that being said, he in turn is deserving of my respect because he leads by example. Our respect for each other lays a foundation for other values as well like communication. Most people may not look at communication as a standard for loving someone but if you really think about it, it's crucial.

In loving another person, you have to be able to communicate all your emotions. All your thoughts, feelings, actions and emotions are conveyed by your ability to communicate effectively. As I stated earlier, I'm a huge communicator. I've never been shy of expressing my love or disappointments. In loving a man, he needs to be able to reciprocate that for me.

There is nothing worse than loving someone and you can't get them to communicate what may be bothering them, or what even empowers them or makes them happy. So many of us are brought up without effective communication. I say effective because communication has to be done with respect and thoughtfulness. Many of us communicate our feelings through yelling, cussing and throwing things. Or some people don't communicate at all. Which for me is just as painful. I can't have a productive relationship with you if you can't communicate well with me. I also can't tolerate a man shutting down on me.

Though, I do understand that some people need to take a breather before they talk about issues or concerns. Our disappointment and anger may put us here. But to go days and not speak to me or act like the problem no longer exists, is a no no for me. At some point we have to be able to address our problems and concerns, find a solution and move forward. That's maturity. I'm a very confrontational person, so in general I work well with a man that is able to address issues and concerns from the jump. The cussing, yelling and gloves off communication doesn't work for me. At this stage of my life, if I even have to raise my voice to you then I'm reevaluating our relationship.

You want to be with someone who can't stand not talking to you and can't stay mad at you. It's too painful for them and for you as well. They're as loyal to your feelings as they are to their own. Loyalty for me is paramount. We have to be able to be in trenches together and be able to count on each other. Again, when life gets's crazy and people get in your ear, your loyalty will keep you bonded. Which if the loyalty is there, no one can get in your ear about your man or your woman anyway. Loyalty denotes permanency. Meaning I'm in it for the long haul with you. That I'm devoted to you and this love that we have for each other. It's that Bonnie and Clyde love that keeps us committed to each other.

Loyalty also represents a binding truth that no matter what happens, I have your back and I'm there for you. There is a bond of trust between us that no one can come between. Trust is a requirement. It is the foundation of a love that lasts for years to come. Trust is earned and as many of you know, it cannot be bought or replaced. It's priceless. The time and energy you put into a person in allowing trust to cultivate between the two of you is irreplaceable.

When the person you love offers their trust and has instilled trust in you, that has to be respected above all costs because once trust is compromised it can never be the same. It loses its value. When trust is lost or damaged, expect loyalty and respect to join it soon after. As human beings, the reality is we are not perfect. We are going to make mistakes. But rest assured that though someone you love may forgive you, your actions or words will never be forgotten and the foundation that was once solid will have a crack in it. It's just never the same when trust is undermined so you have to treat it with reverence.

The reason we are able to love another quite simply is because we are able to trust them. Love itself is built upon this very principle. What's love without trust? They go hand in hand. In giving and receiving trust, your friendship with each other is allowed to grow and to flourish.

I'm not sure many of us realize how important having a friendship with your partner is. My man needs to be my best friend. Hands down. He's the person I share my inner most feelings and dreams with. I share my body with him. There is no better feeling than getting in bed at night and having those pillow talks with the man you love. Having that friendship is a connector and for me, a safe haven. When things get out of hand, I'm a woman to run to my man for guidance and protection. Our friendship with each other is a safe place for me. It's like running to your daddy when you're hurt and you just need that comfort. I feel supported.

Support is a principle that admittedly wasn't always present in my previous relationships. I've always been a very supportive woman. In my past relationships, this is a factor that I longed for. Having the support of the man you love is empowering. You feel like you can conquer the world and any goal because he is there supporting you and cheering you on. We have to be supportive of each other to grow.

As a strong woman, I look to my man to be an aspiration. There have to be qualities in him that inspires me to be better and to want to obtain more not only for my personal growth but for us as a couple. A good man or woman will empower you. Challenge you. Call you on your shit when you're wrong. They will push you beyond your comfortability. Sometimes our loved one see's our potential more than we do. So when we are feeling insecure or questioning our talents or ambitions they're the person that gives us that spark of inspiration for us to operate at our absolute best. Their honesty allows you to confront fears, doubts and insecurities.

One thing about Shanda, honesty is a must. One of my favorite sayings is "Give it to me straight, no chaser!" I can only operate from a place of truth. I can handle the truth. Any man that is lucky enough to one day have me, has to realize always keep it 100 with me. I'm not an over reactor and nine times out of ten most shit doesn't surprise me.

As I've matured my reaction to things tends to be for me to absorb, process and proceed. With that being said, I have no room for untruths. Now a little white lie I can excuse. Like, if you told me you took out the garbage and you didn't. But, significant lies? No. My tolerance is at zero for that. Even in terms of dating. If you represent yourself one way to me, and in time I see it's the opposite, my reaction is "There you are!" I give a man the opportunity to hang himself with me.

Now, I say this in a way that men should equally hold a woman to this standard as well. When a person presents one way and you find out they're someone else, then you need to be proactive in deciding if this is someone you really want in your life or not. Which is why honesty and truth is so important in loving someone. You're getting the real of who they are. No representatives. You don't need to change them. You love them for who they are. You are committed to them.

Our commitment to the person we love should be unwavering. Commitment is strength. This is the part of love that is the muscle to me. Commitment is the action and love is the feeling and sentiment connected to the action. Being in love with someone puts you in the action of wanting to be committed to them. Honestly this is a part of love that is challenging for some people. You can love a person and not be fully committed to them. A part of you still longs for stimulation outside of your relationship.

Commitment and love are like friends and enemies for some people. It can be scary for some men to commit to one woman. This is a truth that many men have openly admitted to me. Commitment is the component that is the hardest thing for them to give. A man's ego and his dedication to keeping his heart and feelings in check won't always allow him to commit.

Commitment is confrontation. It is the place that love expects you to be accountable. If you're not ready for commitment then you're not fully ready for love because your partner is going to assume that your commitment is fully there. Commitment itself is all or nothing. You can't half step it. You are either in or you're not. This will keep a lot of men at bay with a woman he has deep feelings and affection for. He knows her expectations and believes she's worthy of them but knows he may not be able to fully commit to her alone.

I believe what most people won't openly admit to is that commitment over time is challenging. There are hard truths that come with love and when you look at it in a matured way it's easy to understand that love is not for the weak. Being in love takes work. The trust, loyalty, honesty, all the things discussed in this chapter we have to put the effort into it to sustain all its components.

This is why it's so crucial for us to allow ourselves the novelty of enabling love to grow organically. Let the relationship take its course and not rush any of the components. What I've learned over time if the love is real, it will grow without much effort from the two of you. It won't feel like work.

All the principles feel right to both of you and you enjoy fulfilling them for each other. Ultimately we all wish to be loved. Even the most hardened individuals wish to obtain it. I don't care how tough you act or how many "bitches" a man may say he has, at some point when your ass starts getting old you're going to yearn for that one person who will accept you completely and love you for who you are. Multiple women and the player lifestyle will only sustain a man for so long.

I'm a hopeless romantic and truly believe that there is someone out there for each and every one of us. We have to be patient and not let loneliness rush us into the wrong type of people and relationships. Loneliness has sabotaged happiness for many of us. We've settled and allowed negativity to take place in our love lives because the fear of being alone was bigger than us being patient and waiting for the right person that's going to make us happy.

What I've been blessed to learn that even through all my mistakes and mishaps with love, I've come to a place of peace with it. I'm ok with it taking its time with "getting" back to me. I know what I want and what I'm deserving of and I'm not willing to compromise at this point of my life. Love has to come with passion for me because when I'm in love, I love with gusto. I live my life passionately and my love has to be represented with passion as well.

Everything I'm feeling, my man has to match it or exceed it. We have to be passionate and lustful for each other. As importantly for me, we have to have great sexual chemistry. I'm a woman who wants to live in the "honeymoon period" throughout the extent of my relationship.

I live off of excitement and spontaneity. Maybe I'm a dreamer! What I do believe is that the right man is out there for me and I'm ok with waiting. But, when he finds me he better strap on because I'm one helluva ride!! The beauty of love given the right person, they will enliven you. They will fulfill you in ways that you never thought possible. Empower you to your full potential. Everything you need is right in front of you. You are accepted as you are and that in and of itself is LOVE.

CHAPTER 7
HANDLE WITH CARE

"Stand by your man. Give him two arms to cling to and something warm to come home to." – Tammy Wynette

The Independent Woman. She is the source of inspiration and empowerment for women everywhere. She is an implied example of free will, equality and sovereignty. As we are all fully aware, the roles of women have drastically changed and evolved over the years. The days of June Cleaver and domesticity seem light years gone.

In my diligence in finding what men really want and look for in a woman, it was clear the Independent Woman was high on the list in what a man looks for in a woman. She is not intimidating to him, but a reflection of himself in terms of accomplishment and potential. Even with all that she has to offer, a man still appreciates the balance of domestic qualities in a woman as well. They love and appreciate a woman that can cook, clean and tend to them.

The qualities of the 1950's housewife still hold substance in this modern era.

Men are not always quick to openly express their feelings towards wanting a domesticated woman. Quite frankly they're not up to the ridicule of the opinionated woman's spirited backlash that her role is not to just cook, clean and screw him. Truth is many a man would appreciate just that. They do love a woman that can not only cook her ass off, but is also willing to make his plate and pour his drink. There is a comfort and peace in knowing that after a long day of work and difficult people that a man steps into his home with dinner waiting for him. One of the biggest questions of the day your man will ask you is "Babe, what's for dinner?"

Men look to us women to anticipate their needs. It's a quality that has long been lost because it can often be misconstrued as meekness or being submissive. Being able to tap into your man's needs is a quality that men adore about a woman. He doesn't need to ask for anything because you got him covered. This is a component of your relationship that's so important because it taps into you really knowing your man and providing the things he needs that make him feel secure and yes, even spoiled.

As I've shared earlier, I love spoiling a man. I'm a nurturer by nature, so anticipating a man's needs is intrinsic for me. I love doing the little things for a man, that are great to his heart. As "creatures of comfort" they love anything that caters to them feeling relaxed and at ease and that pampers them. So, I'm going to share some of my gems with you ladies that I'm positive your man will appreciate and enjoy!

First, run him a nice warm bath adding a little Epsom salt and lavender oil to it. The Epsom salt assists in relieving minor muscle soreness and achiness. The lavender oil is an essential oil with a host of benefits that help in relieving such things like anxiety and insomnia. It has wonderful relaxation properties.

Now, if your man likes to listen to sports or music you can get one of those little radios that's water resistant for him to listen to while he's relaxing. I suggest one of these types of radios because the last thing he needs is for his phone or headphones to be destroyed by the water. Ask him if he's comfortable and even if he wants a drink while he's taking his bath. Now, while he is enjoying his bath time, you can surprise him with heating his towel. While he's in the tub, just run the towel in the dryer for a few minutes. Believe me, when he gets out that tub and has that warm towel wrapped around him it's going to send him to heaven and back!

Now, once he's all dried off, you have the honor of lotioning his body for him. Front to back. Do it almost as if you're giving him a massage. Let him lay on a separate towel because you don't want the lotion or oil you use to destroy your bedding. This is a move that men find addictive like crack. Honestly. You will send him to sleep with his thumb in his mouth. Another gem I love to do is a head and shoulder massage.

Now, what you're going to do is sit up straight against your headboard. Have your man, with his back to you sit between your legs. This position allows him to relax and lean back into you. Now if your man has hair what you can do is take a comb and part it in small sections. Allow the teeth of the comb to lightly scratch his scalp. Make sure you cover his whole head.

If he doesn't prefer the comb method, you can use your fingers to softly massage through his hair. This will probably have him moaning and groaning. Some men may wish you to lightly grease or oil their scalp while you do this as well. Once the head massage is done, go into lightly massaging his shoulders and back of his neck. Not too strong because this is all about kicking back and honestly bonding in comfort with him.

Now if your man has low hair, what I like to use is a wide brush with soft bristles. Take the brush and just lightly brush his hair in the direction of his hair growth. Use very gentle and soft strokes. If your man is bald, again you can massage him with the very soft and gentle stroking of your fingers. Work your way down his neck and repeat.

The key to it all goes back to anticipating his needs and knowing what he wants and what makes him happy. Believe me ladies a spoiled man is a happy man. What I love as a woman, ask yourself what can you bring to your man that's different than the women before you? You'll be surprised at how your man may react to certain things because he's not use to them or that he never experienced this type of treatment before. It makes them feel special and adored when you go the extra mile in taking care of him. Even if you've been together many years, there are always ways to try something different, no matter how small that can change the climate of your relationship in a positive way.

Now, as much as a man may adore the treatment you delve out to him, he wants to see you treat yourself with even more care. As I've stated before, men are very visual beings. They want a woman that not only presents herself well in terms of her grammar and intellect, but they definitely want a woman that physically attracts them as well. It's not superficial, which is what I know you may be thinking. I want you to think of it this way. Men love a beautiful car. They love riding through and having every man envying his ride. They're aware that their whip represents them as an individual. Believe me when I tell you, they want their woman to equally represent them in the same manner.

Of course, you have more value than a car. I don't want you to take this too far left. What I want to say and very delicately, that as women we have to always be mindful of our appearances and bodies. This is a tough subject for many of us women because our appearance and weight affects us greatly emotionally. Let's talk about the weight issue. In terms of men and what they like, there is no blanket appearance of what attracts them. Their attractions are as diverse as fingerprints. Some men love larger women, some prefer smaller woman. Some like them curvy and some athletic and lean. It is all about preference. Now, as a woman, whatever size you represent my opinion is that you represent it well with your confidence and your appearance. Even if you're at a weight that you're not comfortable with, present yourself in a way that makes you feel beautiful about yourself.

For many women struggling with their weight and body confidence, it can be a struggle to do so because you're not happy with how your body looks. But, here is where you have to be very mindful of your insecurities. You cannot continuously complain and judge your body in a negative light over and over. You will slowly erode your man's confidence in you sexually because your continual self-doubt that you're bringing into the bedroom. He can find you beautiful in his eyes but if you keep proclaiming your faults he's not even going to believe he can satisfy you.

When you let go of your appearance, and this is male or female, and no longer put in the effort self-confidence, don't be surprised that your partner may give up with you. We as individuals set the example on how others treat and view us by how we treat ourselves. Our weight shouldn't define us, but when we have weight issues it's very difficult to separate it. If you're not happy with how you're looking be proactive in changing it and really stick to it. I share this through personal experience. I was a size 22 and at 5'3" it was extremely difficult for me to feel beautiful and confident. In changing my diet and unhealthy lifestyle, I changed not only physically but mentally as well.

You have to get tired of being in a state that doesn't provide you being emotionally healthy. As my mom would say, "When you get sick and tired of being sick and tired you'll do what you need to do." I believe that when it comes to our men and our physical appearance, it's important that we set our own standards. As women, we can easily get caught up into ideals in how we should look physically. It can take a heavy emotional toll on us. That insecurity itself can ruin or undermine the intimacy you share with your man. As I stated previously, bringing your insecurities into the bedroom doesn't allow for your complete freedom. You have to be confident and assured. It doesn't always happen overnight but what I've learned is to allow the process to happen.

If it's something positive in your life expect that it may come with some pain, but allow yourself the novelty of growth and full potential. Ultimately anyone who loves you and sees you going through a struggle will be supportive in you changing in a way that makes you feel capable and empowered. If the proper love is there, so will the support. As we wish to be supported we have to be equally supportive as well. We all know the saying behind every great man is a great woman. I believe this to be unequivocally true.

As a supportive and loving woman I believe a man can reach heights he never imagined. Being in a marriage or relationship your support of each other is what sustains you to reach higher emotionally, physically and even financially. Having an unwavering belief in your man will not only challenge him, but empower him as well. Not all of us have had the gift of our parents or family believing in us. So when we find a partner that cares and pushes us beyond our comfortability that's truly a blessing.

Men ultimately need to feel supported. Their biggest fear is rejection. We have to believe in them enough to state our opinions even if it may not align directly with his. We often times may see a bigger picture than they do. In dealing with their own insecurities or past failures, you may be that light of encouragement to get him to dust his knees off and back into the game. Your support for the most part should be constant. Now, this is within reason of course. If he's trying to open up a meth lab in the basement, then y'all both no better than that! We have to keep it clean ladies!

Which brings me to our next "wish list" conversation. Keeping a clean and tidy home. Ladies, this is not a judgement but I will say in doing my interviews there are a lot of men out here that are not happy with the state of their woman's housekeeping duties or lack thereof. A man wants to come home to a nice, clean house. The last thing any man wants to step into is a shit storm of a home. Dishes not done, clothes everywhere, laundry piled up. If you are a stay at home mom, and your man is out there working his ass off to keep the lights on, in my opinion, your home should be well taken care of. What are you doing all day that the house is out of control?

I know this is a very touchy subject for some women. If you are working hard and have a demanding career being able to keep all the balls in the air regarding wife, home and children are a lot to take on. So in addressing this topic, if you're just being lazy please expect that your man will have a real problem with you, as he should. If there is no real substantial reason why your home is not clean and together than I can't advocate that. But, if you both have careers that challenge you being able to keep things together then maybe these duties can be shared to balance the responsibility. Either way, a man's home is his castle and the last thing he wants is a dirty one!

For every woman reading this who keeps her home in order, please believe me when I tell you it's one of the things your man loves about you. Men do judge a woman on how well she keeps her home and her children. If you're a single mom out there dating and your children are not kept well, a man will look at you sideways. He may not openly admit it to you, but your children looking unkempt makes you look neglectful. There is nothing more of a turn-off than to see a woman that looks great and her children are looking uncared for. It's just not cool.

I have witnessed this kind of nonsense with my own eyes. Our children are representative of our care. They are a reflection of our commitment to mothering them and doing what's best for them. Being a mother is the most important job in the world. If your mothering skills leave a lot to be desired expect that number one, keeping a good husband will only last so long. He will eventually leave you. Number two, if you're single and he sees how neglectful you are with your children it will turn him off.

If he doesn't care, and you two still find love than y'all asses deserve each other and the kids need to go with their daddy. There is zero tolerance for bad parenting. For the ones that are great at it, again your man takes pride in the fact that you are a good mother to your children. Especially a household that has a blended family. Being good to each other's children and taking care of them like your own will only strengthen the bond of trust between the two of you.

As I shared earlier being raised with my stepfather, I think of how important he was to my life and who I am as a woman today. I've always been grateful for his love and to the important values he instilled in me and my siblings. My mother loved him even more because of how much he loved and cared for us. There's no replacing that. It takes a huge amount of patience and understanding for this type of family to work.

In looking at my own upbringing, I believe the co-parenting worked so well is because my mother trusted my stepfather. She trusted his decisions and believed that he wanted what was best for us. She never undermined his authority and she definitely never let us children know that his respect was less than hers. I've seen and experienced too many occasions when the children are given more respect in decisions than adults. This undermines the validity of the other parent and this is just disastrous.

The understanding that my mother showed laid the groundwork for a trust that strengthened their relationship. In looking at what a man needs, there is no blanket explanation. One man's needs may not be another's. The key to it all is being able to understand him as an individual and allow yourself to not let over judgements and cynicism to erode your belief in him. The nagging, complaining and constant attitude doesn't help in providing a loving relationship for either of you.

A woman's attitude has the capacity to make or break his affection towards her. I'm not sure if enough of us women realize how important it is to check ourselves and our own behavior towards the men we love. They reflect or react to what we put forth also. One thing for sure is that all men need the love of a woman who is patient and understanding. Understanding that he's not perfect, there will be times he's gonna fuck up. But be understanding enough to know that ultimately his track record speaks for itself and that you accept him as he is and handle him with care!

"Demanding my privacy doesn't mean I'm hiding something."
                                    -Justin Murphy

CHAPTER 8
WE ARE FAMILY

"The strength of a nation derives from the integrity of the home." - Confucius

The bosom of family represents our first introduction to love. How we love and how comfortable we are with love starts here. When we become adults everything that we've learned, and experienced through family is a guiding force in how we view the world and our relationships. For many of us the representation, if you're blessed was a good one. But for every great family out there, there are some that leave much to be desired. Anyone that truly knows me knows how important family is to me. I grew up in a home where my parents reiterated our love and respect for each other as individuals as well as us as a family unit.

My parents were very big on us being an entirety. As a family, birthdays were celebrated with all of us coming together and enjoying each other. Holidays were celebrated with lots of food, music and good times. My mother and her siblings were extremely close. My aunts and uncles felt more like second mothers and fathers. To this day my aunts are like my mother. My uncle, like a father. Our cousins more like siblings to all of us as well. Growing up that's just how it was.

My parents did a great job of instilling that closeness and bond that we have to this day. When I became a mom, I knew one of the most important qualities that I wanted to instill in my daughter was that same strong bond of family. It was important that everything my parents did right with me that I imbue those qualities in her. Even though I had my daughter at 15, I've always been a responsible and loving parent to her. The foundation of what my parents imparted in me allowed me to take on motherhood with maturity and responsibility.

In being a young mother, I knew I wanted my daughter to have a wonderful relationship with her father. I knew how important her father's role in raising our daughter would be. I wanted her to have that bond like I did with my stepfather. Young himself, at 16 her dad took to parenting the way that I did. He was great at spending quality time with her and also being very affectionate and loving to her. She never needed anything because he always was present in that way in providing well for financially and emotionally. We both were very responsible with her and loved her beyond measure.

By the time my daughter turned 7 I saw a shift in her father and his commitment to parenting. Weekends he was supposed to pick her up, he didn't. Holidays he became absent. No gifts or acknowledgement. My baby would pack her little bag and wait for her dad and he'd be a no show. If you've ever been through this as a parent, you know how hard it is to see your children go through the pain of disappointment and rejection. It was very difficult for me and I cannot begin to tell you in enough words what this put me through as a mother.

I knew that as a mom I could only provide so much emotionally. I couldn't replace her father. But, I thank God for my mother's wisdom. My anger had me at a level that was beyond reasoning. My conversations with my mother helped me in raising my daughter in a way that I could be proud of even to this day. I will share with you even through every hurtful phase that my child went through, I NEVER at any time bad mouthed her father to her. Not one unkind word. What I did tell her is that "One day your dad is going to need you." That was it.

My feeling at the time was what could I say to her that he hasn't already shown through action? My mother taught me long ago, you don't have to say anything. Just sit back and watch. I made a promise to myself that she would never hear me speak a bad word about her father because I didn't want the blame for any view she had of him. It was so important for me to share this because many of us have to deal with the situation of an ex and our children and co-parenting. Breaking up in and of itself is a very painful process. Adding children to the equation takes it to a whole other level.

As a woman, what is important for me to share is that when we are no longer present in or ex's life in a romantic way I know that we can carry anger and resentment. We can still be reeling from how and why the breakup took place. It's a natural feeling. You share children with a person that has hurt you and that can be devastating to say the least. This person for all intent and purposes will always be a part of your life in some way because you share the blood of your children between the two of you. What's important to understand is to not allow the anger and resentment that you carry for him overshadow what is best for your children.

There has to be some form of civility between the two of you so your children can still feel protected and loved despite the dissolution of their parent's relationship. Your children should never be used as pawns or as a means of control. As a woman, you can't keep a good father from his children because he sucked at being a husband or boyfriend to you. You should never speak ill of the other parent to your children nor should your children be brought into the adult's situation.

Your children should not be commenting on what's going on between their parents. They should not even be privy to adult conversations at all. Even if you have to go outside in your car to have a private conversation, your children should see a minimal amount of disagreements in front of them. If your children are teens, even more so, you should not be discussing your marriage or relationship issues with them in a way like you're needing their advice or commentary from them to substantiate your anger. This puts them in the position of choosing sides as well as them thinking it's ok for them to make comments about an adult situation. Your children feel they can make comments, suggestions and remarks because you brought them into it. Once you do that, it's hard to come back from that.

I know this is challenging and you may be ready to throw this book in a corner somewhere saying I don't understand. Believe me I do. It's important that we as parents consistently let our children know that aside from what the adults are going through, that they're going to be fine. We have all seen and maybe experienced these situations. It is hard as hell to take the high road because it challenges our emotions. But anger can put us in crazy situations that can escalate an already tumultuous stage. Many times we can't come back from certain things being said or situations happening. It's important to not let our emotions get the best of us where it puts us in a place of vulnerability.

In the subject of co-parenting, it may be best to even view your relationship with your ex that it's not about me and you anymore, but what's best for our children. A whole new relationship with the different view of just the children may be what's needed. If the idea of the two of you as parents getting along is not feasible then it's important that a third party that you both trust becomes involved that may assist in making your situation less volatile. Whatever has to be done, the process for your children should be as painless as possible. I believe over time, once the anger subsides and you learn to move on past the hurt in your relationship the idea of being civil to each other becomes more of a reality. Moving forward emotionally in a positive way in the long run allows you a better opportunity to find someone that is better suited for you.

Once you've moved on, and you feel that you're ready to begin dating, as a mom you have to be very responsible in whom you expose your children to and whom you have your children around. Dating and your children require responsibility and tact. Having a new person in your life is one thing but having them in your children's lives takes on a whole other meaning.

In my strong opinion, I believe someone you are casually dating should never really be introduced to your children. Younger children form attachments quite easily and if this is a man that you're not positive is going to be a permanent fixture in your life then he should not be introduced to your child or children. A man that's responsible himself will know the right time to be introduced to your children as well. If he's serious about you and in love with you, and he's ready to take on the responsibility of being a part of your children's lives is definitely a conversation that you both should have and an understanding you both come to.

Another important concern I want to bring up is the quality of the man that you expose to your children. Be a good judge of character to see if they're even worthy enough to be around your children. You can't expose your children to a man that doesn't have himself together and in turn is setting a bad example. Drinking, partying and sexing around your kids ain't cool either. I'm not being "Judgemental Judy" but I want to keep it real in acknowledging that some women out here are real loose with their kids and very irresponsible. I'm a huge advocate of a man raising his children if the mother does not have her shit together.

Your children can't afford the mistake of your bad judgement. There have been too many horror stories of children being beaten, raped or killed because they were unprotected by irresponsible parenting. There is no room for error here. You have to be very mindful that your choices become their life and can affect them greatly. With correct judgement and timing having the right relationship can be a positive experience not only for you but your children additionally.

In deciding to move forward with your relationship and taking it to the next level, having the blended family becomes either a blessing or a curse to your relationship or marriage. Let's start at the beginning. As a step-parent, the role you play in your stepchildren's lives will stay with them forever. Be it a positive or negative experience. It's important, I believe that you convey that you're not trying to replace a parent, but your role is to guide them as one. As much as we may love our stepchildren you have to be honest with yourself of their view of you. Certain children will always carry an affinity to their biological parent even if that parent is neglectful. They may even always wish for their biological parents to get back together no matter how good you may be to them. It just is what it is.

The reality is that your stepchildren will not love you right away and may even not fully like you. Don't set too high an expectation of your relationship with your stepchildren. Your relationship needs time to be cultivated through trust, care, respect and communication. I've always felt that the position of a stepparent is to be a friend and an ear of support and guidance. In looking to achieve love and like from your step-children you should never go too far out of bounds of parent and child. You can't try to buy their affection or be too lenient with them in winning their love. You want those feelings to come over time naturally because they respect you.

Spend quality time with them and get to know them as individuals by showing interest and support of what they love and like to do. Be patient and understanding that your own feelings towards them as well need time to develop. There may be one child you feel closer to than the other. Be honest with your partner if you're feeling out of place or feeling that what you're doing is not enough. Here is where you both have to have the understanding and agreement that we can openly speak about each other's children even if it's negative. Done in the boundaries of respect, you have to communicate your feelings good and bad.

It's important to acknowledge each other's concerns and issues. As parent's we are naturally very protective of our children and for some of us you can't tell us anything about our kids. But that mindset doesn't allow you to have an objective view because your children are not always perfect. And because they're children doesn't mean it's an excuse for their behaviors. My thinking is very old school. It's more important for me to be a parent and making the tough decisions that they may not agree with, but they have to respect them. I'm also a disciplinarian. Meaning my children are held accountable for their behavior.

Children need boundaries and as parents it's our job to establish them. It's necessary because it shows our children that we care. As a stepparent in establishing discipline you don't want to always come off as the enforcer but your partner, has to be right there alongside of you handing out the discipline. The important part is that the children always have to be respectful of the role you have decided to take on in raising them. As a couple, you have to have a clear understanding in how you both wish to raise each other's children. Parent's in my belief, have to always be on the same page. You have to have a discussion on how the kids are to be disciplined, chore responsibilities, school, house rules, friends, boyfriends, everything! All that has to be agreed upon together and there has to be a clear understanding that together we're stronger, divided we're weak. You have to always present yourselves and follow through as a united front.

As I stated in the previous chapter, children will look for holes and crevices in their parent's relationships. If they find one parent weaker than the next, they will try to get their way or manipulate one parent against the next. And it's normal that they'll do this because all children want their way. The key is that as parents you stay one step ahead of them. What's important to truly understand regarding a blended family is that you have to consistently reiterate yourselves as one family.

Meaning as a new family you want to establish your own traditions together. If it's we all sit down at dinner together at a certain hour and we commune about each other's day. Or we celebrate our birthdays together. Or as a family there's an activity you all do as one. It may be tough for some of your children to get use to, but as a new family you have to be able to create those bonds as a unit as soon as it feels right. Younger children will take to a new stepparent rather quickly. Pre-teens and teenagers it's going to be much harder to bring them into the fold, but again don't set your expectations too high too soon. You'll hurt yourself emotionally if you're looking for things to go a certain way and they haven't as yet.

The importance of setting your own traditions over time is that what once felt like "them and us" now feels only like family. Separatism can erode the fabric of your family and if as parent's you allow too much of that expect that the fabric starts to come apart. It's vital as a couple that you support each other's decisions with the kids. One child's needs or wants can't be greater than the next. If something is going to compromise what you've worked hard to build together as a family, then it needs to be evaluated. Some children will try to buck this new family system, but for it to last you have to stay the united front. At all costs.

Also, it's important to know that an ex can cause major damage to your new life and family that you're trying to establish. As much as you work hard to provide a wonderful environment for your family be prepared that there may be others that are pissed with your new situation. Their resentment and anger can have them trying to undermine your relationship with your stepchildren. They may even go so far as to bad mouth you and instill hatred towards you and their ex. It's a mess, but believe me when I tell you, I know exactly what I'm talking about.

Let's talk about the ex and dealing with your stepchildren's other parent. For certain situations, it is best to have your man deal directly with his ex. If she's a woman that you have low regard for and you know she can make you come out of character, then it's best that you have very little dealings with her. Let your man deal with her. Ideally you want to be able to have that Russell Simmons and Kimora Lee family bond going on, but unfortunately not everyone has the capacity for that type of maturity. Some men quite honestly have to deal with the "baby momma" from hell. I hate even saying that word, but to me it's a mentality.

Certain women that men share a child with will have him feeling like he was given a death sentence. He has to deal with this woman that he has no respect for because of her lack of good parenting. This is why it's so important that we take a long hard look at who we get in bed with. These people have the ability to affect the rest of your life because you have a child with them.

And this is where you men have to take notice. You have to wrap your lil' head up. You can't be letting loose in loose women and expect that a baby isn't possible. We've seen enough Maury Show's to know better than that! If you're sleeping with a woman that you are casually fucking, you should be using a condom. If you're looking to become parents with this woman then ok, that's a whole other deal. The reality is that man or woman we have to look at our choices and realize that they can greatly affect the course of our lives. Your ex and your new woman may not get along, but as a man you have to handle your situation responsibly.

Of course you're going to go to your new woman and complain about your last one and vice versa. But, sharing children with your ex, it's important as a man that you set boundaries with her as well and let her know what's not cool for her to do. Communication is key because then there's no guesswork. If you're lucky and all three of you can sit down and discuss the children and getting along cohesively than that's great. God Bless this ability. If this is not doable then again certain boundaries have to be set that everyone can agree to because what's most important is that the children are made to feel loved and cared for by both sets of parents.

Your extended family also has to understand that your new life is an adjustment with them as well and they have to respect boundaries. Grandmothers, grandfathers, aunts, and uncles will all have a say. There will be a ton of comments, opinions, thoughts and feelings. With that being said, you may have to speak to these relatives regarding boundaries and what's best for you as a couple.

If there's a situation that family members are doing that allows negativity then it has to be addressed. People getting into your relationship and situation can cause new problems that neither of you needs. No one wants the pressure and headache of family members not respecting boundaries. Some family members may have to be put in their place. You may have to sit down with them and explain why you feel a certain way or how a situation can make you uncomfortable.

As a couple, you both have to always talk about your

feelings and allow yourselves the notion that things are not going to always be perfect. Everything in building your family is going to come with some opinion and negativity. Expect that. If you rely on each other's faith that ultimately what's best for your family is by what you two put into it, then combining your families can be a loving experience for all of you. And, with all your hard work things still are a struggle then don't hesitate to get outside help like a family therapist. Some people may need the help of an outside and objective opinion. Some families may greatly benefit from professional support so don't be embarrassed if that's the case. What's important to understand here is that when you begin this process of combining your families, it's easy to put all your focus on your children because you want their transition to be as comfortable as possible.

Many couples forget to focus on their intimate relationship in order to keep everyone else happy. You have to continually feed each other emotionally now more that ever because of all the other demands. It's important not to lose sight of each other. In my personal memories and how my stepfather played such a huge role for me, I'm grateful that I had him in my life. My mother chose well and in her good judgement it allowed me the pleasure of being loved by the first man I ever loved. I have spoken of him often throughout my book because he inspired my love and appreciation of men.

We all know how important family plays into our lives. Whether a biological parent, stepparent or adoptive parent, family is family. Done right, they are representative of our first love.

CHAPTER 9
BECAUSE I'M HAPPY

"The purpose of our lives is to be HAPPY"- Dalai Lama

"Unicorns and rainbows." This is Shanda's feel good quote. When a situation threatens to take me out of my character I just repeat these three words and it centers me. Some people chant, some meditate, others pray. Whatever we have to do to allow happiness to take place, it's important that we allow it to be a guiding force in our lives. Happiness is a brick in the foundation of love. I'm not sure if many people even equate love to happiness. But, how great can love be without it?

Ask a woman if she loves a man, and her first response will be "Yes, he makes me so happy!" For so many of us, the word love is often associated with pain. At some vulnerable points in our lives, the pain and the love has gone hand in hand. That trait of pain may even be more dominant for some because they've never honestly experienced a love that made them feel truly happy. One thing that I've learned is that in order for you to receive a love that feels right and just to you, you have to have an inner happiness and peace within yourself.

With this being a guide for women, it was really important to me that we have the discussion of personal happiness. If I had the opportunity to sit with you alone and ask you one on one if you're happy what would you tell me? Or, if I asked you what makes you happy could you give me definitive answers? You'd be surprised in knowing so many women would say no, I'm not happy. And admittedly, not have a clear awareness of what actually makes them happy. Having an awareness and clear view of our happiness allows us the foundation of knowing and taking pride in what kind of relationship we deserve and who deserves us. When you have that kind of clarity, it sets a standard that you won't compromise.
In truth we work hard for our happiness. Because life's job is to continuously throw us curves, it can compromise our ability to be emotionally receptive to happiness. Circumstances and situations beyond our control can deeply affect our state of happiness and wellbeing. It can take effort to keep smiling when it seems like your world is coming apart. It becomes easier to be angry and to lash out.

In opening the "angry" discussion, we are all fully aware if we address the elephant in the room, that culturally we are stereotyped as women. Caucasian and Asian women are considered meek, docile and understanding. African American women are considered angry, always having an attitude, smart mouth, and opinionated. Maybe there's some truth in it all. As an African American woman myself if you asked my ex's if I fell into any of those "types" they'd say yeah, that's Shanda. I openly admit to my anger being an issue for me

at one point. I've also been known for my smart mouth and opinionated attitude most of my life.
Listen, I look at it as a sign of intelligence but my ex saw it as me being a smart ass. Tomato. Toe mot toe! It's all about perception! But, getting back to the discussion in seriousness, we have to be mindful of our attitudes and our behavior. As I shared in the very beginning, it can be hard for a man to love a woman with so much anger and negativity within her. It's almost next to damn near impossible. Whatever has us in that state we have to be mature enough to look it in the mirror and admit that we have to pull it together and be proactive in changing our behavior for the better. You can't expect a man to treat you like an orchid when you behave like a snapdragon! A man can't water this kind of woman, because she's not even in a state of growth.

When you think of it objectively, what kind of man is going to be attracted to a cussin', loud, angry, and stankin' attitude woman? The reality is you attract what you put out. More than likely the type of man that will put up with this type of woman is going to be just as angry himself and they'll both just be horrible mirrors of each other. Or you're dealing with a man who's balls have never seen the light of day because his woman has snatched them from him and put them in her panties!
I can't tell you how many times I've witnessed with my own eyes women going in on they men out in public. I can't stand to see a man with no strength in him to stand up to his woman. It's weakness and that's not attractive at all. A woman can't respect a man that allows her to disrespect and walk all over him.

All this craziness comes at a heavy price. Our children become privy to it and this type of behavior and personalities, as I stated before can go on for generations. Nothing good comes from any of this. Which is why at some point of awareness and maturity and yes even spiritual growth you have to address your issues. In general, I hate using that word, but a lot of us out here do have some serious issues!

A huge culprit is abandonment. Abandonment is when we experience an oversensitivity and over reaction to our partner's withdrawal or perceived withdrawal to us for whatever reason. We get bat shit crazy or we're on ten for no real reason or we take a very small issue to a level that it has no place being. Abandonment and the effects it has on an individual will rob most couples of experiencing a trusting and loving relationship. This issue may go all the way back to parents who were not there for their children, or to an ex that didn't do right by you. It comes with so many different reasons but what I will say is that all of them are potentially harmful to the relationship in general.

The outbursts, overreactions, crying spells, and erratic behavior all have to be addressed so your partner can be free of the chains that this issue puts on them. The bigger picture is that if this is something that you're experiencing don't be ashamed in admitting you need to seek help. I'm a huge advocate of therapy. For years therapy has received a bad rep due to people feeling like it's not necessary. That it's only for "crazy people" That's just not true. Most people with that very opinion in my experience have never even been to therapy. Therapy allows you to sit with a professional that will take the time to listen and go through the layers of your life objectively.

Most of us have gotten our "therapy" from friends and family who quite honestly aren't objective enough or who could use a little therapy they damn selves. There's nothing harmful in seeking outside help in becoming emotionally healthy. In fact, I'm one to believe that not everyone has to even know. Not everything needs to be on blast especially such a delicate subject as therapy.

So initially if you're thinking of going, just go and absorb and digest. Once you become a little stronger maybe then you can share that you're going. Either way as an adult, we have to be able to be strong enough to admit when we're weak and that we need help. There's no shame in that. I personally have gone to therapy and it was an eye opening experience for me. I admit that even I had my own preconceived notions about therapy. I went in and was transformed and actually looked forward to going again because it was good to let go emotionally and allow someone else to help me.

When you're a strong personality you can build yourself up mentally that you're good, you don't need anyone's assistance. But, if you're noticing a distinct pattern in all your relationships and friendships and it leads back to you and this issue, at some point you have to deal with it. I'm not sure if many of us take a strong look in our patterns in regards to our relationships and even friendships. If you notice a distinct issue or scenario that consistently affects your relationships, it's time to have that one on one conversation with yourself.

For example, if you notice you have a habit of becoming close to someone, bonding with them, then you suddenly pull away, then that has to be addressed. You start to leave a trail of broken hearts and resentment because of your fear of abandonment. You have to consider your need to sabotage your relationships comes from a deeper place and at some point you have to confront those demons. Again, it may very well come from when you were a child and from an issue with one or both your parents. In addressing the parenting issue, as parents we have to realize that how we raise our children and what we show them in terms of love, affection, and communication will play a huge role in the type of relationships they will have as adults.

I have met so many men in doing this book, that admit to not being raised with much affection, attention, love, and acknowledgement. And many of us women have as well. But as a woman, and if you've been here you can appreciate what I'm about to say, it is very difficult to love a man who doesn't know how to accept your affection, attention, love and communication because he wasn't brought up with it and doesn't know how to express himself in these matters.

It's almost like we pay the price for their parent's mistakes. I have seen so many people use this as a crutch for emotional detachment in their relationships. "Oh, I wasn't raised like that" or "You know it's hard for me because my mother never did this or my father didn't do that." And equally, men have dealt with many women who have daddy issues. The absentee father has caused many women to be on constant defense in their adult relationships and in turn having a defensive approach to love. Their father's shortcomings or lack of involvement in their daughter's lives leave them feeling leery and distrustful of men and their relationships. You wind up becoming a woman either overcompensating for the lack of a relationship with your father or under compensating for fear of being hurt. Either way, you're scarred and it leaves you bringing these detrimental issues into your adult relationships.

Most women that harbor negative feelings for their father will most assuredly bring those same negative feelings with her to the man in her life in some form or other. Whatever the issue, male or female, these are all valid contributors in who we become as adults and how we operate within our relationships. But again, when we become adults and mature and recognize our shortcomings it is our job to acknowledge them and to do something about them.

You cannot have a person deeply in love with you giving you their all, and you are not able to manifest and express it properly in return. And quite frankly the person that loves you doesn't want to keep hearing the excuses of why you can't give them what they need. They want to see you be proactive in you changing the issue than you just proclaiming the issue. A person can only take so much of this kind of treatment. Resentment will take hold and so the cycle continues. My saying? " Fix it!" If I'm meaningful enough to you, and you say you love me, then fix it. I don't want to hear shit else. I want to SEE you doing what you said you were going to do. We're grown and it's time to get on with life and get on with being emotionally responsible.

One thing that I can't tolerate is grown folk with grown ass excuses. I'm an action- oriented person, so I have to see a man that is strong enough to be loving to me in a way that empowers me and makes me happy. He can't have a reservation based on an issue. And if he does, then he has to be willing to address an issue or concern and change it because he loves me and doesn't want to lose me.

We women have to recognize that as much as we love, we can't love for the both of us. We'll want a man so much that the fear of losing him is too great and we'll convince ourselves that we have enough love for the both of us. It's a fairytale that even Cinderella can't live up to. And frankly, do any of us want to be in a relationship that you continuously have boxing gloves on to maintain? Everything becomes a fight. If you have to regularly fight for your love, affection, and communication why even bother? I strongly believe in couples staying together and working out their issues. But, I'm not an advocate of one person putting in the continual effort and the other doing nothing but the hurting and promising with no real effective change.

We live in a society that gives up too quickly on our relationships and marriages. No one wants to stay when it's time to roll up the sleeves and get their hands dirty. But, in comparison, we have to as individuals stand up for our emotional and mental happiness. If your partner steadily shows you that you're not a priority and neither are your feelings then you have to make some tough decisions. Love and happiness comes with work but if your partner is worthy then it's worth the effort you put not only into them but the relationship as well.
With that being said, let's talk about love and happiness. Couple style. I cannot express how important it is to have fun and enjoy each other. You ever see a couple and you can just tell that they're in love and adore each other? They're always laughing, holding hands or can't keep their hands off each other? They just emit an energy of positivity. You can't fake that. That comes from two people that generally LIKE each other. There are many of us in love with our significant other but don't necessarily like them anymore. You have to like the person you're with just as much as you love them.

Liking your partner means you revel in being around them. You want to dote on them and have fun with them. They're a joy to be around. I think the advent of time can take away from couples enjoying each other. Things can become quite regular and mundane, but you have to take time and enjoy each other outside of everything and everyone else. You have to do things together that you both have a good time doing. And yes, plenty of good sex is up there on the list. Yall already know how I feel about that one! But, it can be going to the movies, going bike riding. Even getting in the car putting on some great music and going for a ride together.

Now, ladies here's the fun part with the driving. While he's driving wear something sexy. It can be a low cut blouse or a dress that shows your legs. But, something in his peripheral that has him looking at you that when yall get home it's going down. But you can tease and touch him a little in the car too! Whatever it is that BOTH of you do together that makes you happy, do it! Laugh together and be a part of each other's lives. Do you know how many couples out here that share the same roof but not the same home? Meaning they're both in different places emotionally. It feels like you're living alone on an island. It's very easy to let life get in the middle and against the two of you. You have to share your space of loving each other emotionally and physically. You can't take your partner's presence for granted.

I had a very good friend that was going through a tough break-up say something so profound to me and I never forgot it. She said the loneliest time she ever had in her life was when she was married to her husband. Think of how significant that statement is. If you are feeling lonely in your relationship or marriage that's a problem. This is where unhappiness lives. This is where things begin to go downhill. When that happiness is gone and the feeling of loneliness takes residence this is your action moment. What are you going to do about it and are you prepared for the follow through of what you need to do?

One thing I've learned about being a person that gives advice is this. People for the most part, innately already know what they need to do. When they're seeking advice, it's generally them desiring an ear in sharing their problem and needing to vent. The hard part of knowing what we need to do comes in the form of action. Are we prepared to deal with the consequences or repercussions that come in making the tough decisions for ourselves?

Many times a strong stand we need to take comes with these two elements. This keeps people at a place of inaction and unhappiness because they're not ready to deal with what honestly needs to be done. This is why at the beginning of this chapter I spoke about how important it is in knowing what our happiness and state of wellbeing means to us. You'll stand up for it and demand it. The right and loving person will stand by you in giving it and supportive of it also.

It's all about that reciprocity loves. Life is short and what I've learned when it comes to love is that, the decision we make in whom we decide to love will be one of the biggest decisions of your life. This person will either empower and inspire you or drain and destroy you. Your decision has to come from a place of knowing what you want and whom you deserve. You have to know your worth and understand that that doesn't come with a price. When we make the wrong decisions in loving someone and allowing years and years to pile on in unhappiness we don't get that time back. It's not like God said "You know what, you made a bad choice in being with this person for 10 years, so I'm going to give you an additional 10 years for your misjudgment." You don't get the privilege of a redo.

So, the time that you have here should be spent on loving someone that is of good choice and judgment. Your time, emotion, love and intimacy is not to be played with. Ain't nobody got time for that! Let the church say amen!! As couples, I believe in moving forward with your lives together, you're going to go through your changes. It will be a roller coaster ride. The kids, finances, family, friends, deaths, losses and gains will all be a part of your journey together. You two will experience it all.

The strength of getting through it all will depend on your ability to find happiness through your ride together. Never forget how and why you fell in love with each other in the first place and all the hard work and sacrifice that you put into each other. Remember to laugh and kiss and make love. Kissing will help a multitude of issues.
I have to discuss kissing real quick. I LOVE kissing. I had to cap love because I'm not sure if people do it enough anymore. Especially couples. Don't just give me a peck on my cheek or a quick kiss on my lips. I'm not your sister or your momma! I want that tongue and that intimate connection that comes with kissing. I want to put my hands on the back of your neck while our tongues are going at it! "Babe, it's what makes me HAPPY!!!"

CHAPTER 10
THE TRUTH OF THE MATTER

"Three things cannot be long hidden: the sun, the moon, and truth."

- Buddha

We are all too familiar with the saying "The truth will set you free." We all know the importance of truth and wish for it in our relationships and friendships. This is one chapter that I hesitated in doing. I had to really sit and think is this information that I want to share because I can't sugar coat and use nice words in conveying my feelings? In the end, I decided to go with it. As much as I love men and this being a Pro Man book it was important for me as a woman to convey truths about men that we women just have to look at and comes to terms with.

Truths that hurt and truths that may not be fair. But, as I kick the elephant out on his ass in our discussion let's get to it. Men love women. A heterosexual male's instinct is to hunt and conquer. As women, the reality is that includes us. If you look at a male lion and how he moves with his women, the human male is not too far removed. A male lion will have different prides and mate and keep it moving.

Many men that we women encounter live their life this way. I don't care how much work, love and time you put into a man if he is not open to you being his only woman, you assuredly will not be his only woman. Men have the strong ability to separate emotion from sexuality. Meaning yes, I love you, but I'll still fuck and conquer if I'm allowed to or while under the radar. Now, not all men fall into this. I'm not making a blanket statement here. There are plenty of men who are monogamous. But, many a man has strayed because of a need and desire to experience something, excuse me, someone different. Men love a new experience. They will desire another woman even knowing they should not. It's like going to Baskin and Robbins. Why experience one flavor when there's so many to choose from?

But bigger than flavor and choice let's openly discuss how men view us women today. I say today because the male view in this generation is a far cry from our parent's and grandparents. I believe honestly that women carried themselves with more respect and class than they do today. It's a hard truth. The type of woman a man fucks and whom he will marry are vastly different. It will depend greatly on how you as a woman carry and present yourself. A man will automatically know by how a woman represents herself where he places her. This woman here, I can fuck her and keep it movin'. This woman here is nice, but she trying to tie me down and I'm not looking for that. This one got good pussy but I don't trust her. This one is pretty but she spoiled and selfish.

Believe me when I tell you ladies, no matter how much of a reputation a man has, he will look at yours and judge you on it. And he will also judge you on your appearance. If everything is hanging out and leaves no imagination, he's going to look at you as being easy. If you have tattoos in certain places, he will judge you on that as well. They will refer to certain tattoos as tramp stamps. If you speak and act in a way that's overtly sexual or your tone and conversation is a certain way, he will judge and categorize you on all these things. To this day, men still expect and hold us women to a higher standard. If you show anything less than what his ideal is, he will privately hold you accountable. He will put you in the categories of "keep her" or "keep it movin'." It's very little gray area. What we women have to understand is that a man's thinking for the most part is very simplistic. It's more cut to the chase. They know exactly what they want and what they don't want.

We make the mistake in thinking we can change their minds. No, we can't. Their minds are made up. We women at one point or other have come face to face with the pain of wanting a man that just didn't want us. No matter how much we've sexed him, cooked for him, sucked his dick, did everything that would make him happy, if he's not ready and prepared for you, it's just not happening. And men for the most part will be honest with a woman. They'll tell us, I'm not looking for a relationship. Translation? I'm not looking for a relationship with YOU. Believe me another woman may come along and he falls head over heels for her. Now his ass is in love. With her. Not you. But we'll still enter into a sexual relationship with them and provide them everything a relationship encompasses, but not get their stamp of approval. Shit, for some women, no one may even know you're seeing each other. He hasn't told anyone of significance about you. He doesn't talk about his family or friends nor does he ask you about yours or anything going on with you because that's too personal. He doesn't want you in that space. Your relationship is based on boundaries that he's set and you agreed to by dealing with him and the insignificant liaison you're having with him. I say it's insignificant because where is this relationship going for you? How has it benefited you emotionally? Are you hurting because he doesn't feel the same way about you?

You can't get mad at him because he was honest with you from the jump. He told you he wasn't looking for a relationship. And right here is where we women make our mistakes. We start the game and think we can change the rules once our emotions come into play. We rush going in thinking it's fun and exciting and he really likes me! No matter how great your qualities or how much you may think you can "sell" him on your great attributes, it doesn't matter. He ain't ready.

I had a man tell me in interview, "Shanda women always wanna change the relationship. They always wanna rush things." We women can be guilty of that. We want to go in with blinders on. You have to be able to look at all sides because a man does. He's going to weigh you and all his options in what's best for him. I don't care if you're astrological chart or horoscope says that ya'll are perfect for each other, it doesn't change the fact that he's not ready for a relationship with you now or never. A man may have another woman all up in his nostrils, but still fuck with you because the one he wants is not giving it up yet or he views her with more respect and wants to court her. But his needs still need to be met and that's where you come in. You have to take the rose colored glasses off and look at your relationships with a clear vision.

The truth is a man will use you for clandestine sex if you allow him to. He will take and take and take until he is no longer in need of you. The problems lie in you needing him. We women have a very hard time of not being able to separate ourselves sexually and emotionally. As much as we may enter a "relationship," saying I'm good, eventually your heart starts to pull at you about this man that is entering your body and that you're spending time with. It's almost a given for us.

Now, there are some women who move just like a man in this respect. She'll be able to sleep with multiple men and keep it moving and keep her emotions intact. The irony in this is all the men this type of woman deals with fall in love with her and she's not about that life. It's crazy. We want what we can't have. And who wants us, we don't want them. In general, men like a challenge when it comes to a woman. If it comes too easy for him, it's not interesting. It's like feeding time at the zoo. The zookeeper puts a rat in a cage with a python. That rat will run around crazy knowing he's gonna get eaten. The python will let that rat go on and on. Only when he's really hungry he will eat that rat. He knows the rat is a given. He doesn't have to work for it because it was thrown in there. When you take away the chase, you take away the excitement. That's how it is with a man.

When you give him everything up front and he ain't have to work for it, watch how quick he'll lost interest in you. I don't care how beautiful you are. How big and wide your ass is, if you give him your "golden lady" without effort, he will partake and keep it moving. We women have to allow not only the chase to happen but the effort. Oh and by the way, the fact that you gave him that pussy so soon, yes, I said the "p" word, he judged you on that. Yeah, he's thinking if he got it so quick, who else did? There goes that double standard. But, believe me, he's judged you and right then and there he put you in either of those two categories.

What we allow from the very beginning sets the tone in the male opinion and view of us women. Let's have the social media conversation. I had a very good male friend of mine tell me how social media has changed the dating scene on a huge scale. If you look at Instagram and other social outlets, women are putting themselves out there for the taking. What use to take work in getting a woman, now you have your pick of women to choose from. You don't even have to leave your home to get hooked up with a woman now. You can like her pics. Tell her to email you her number and it goes from there. There's so many women to choose from and they leave nothing to the imagination anymore. So with all that being handed to you as a man, what makes a man want to or need to go the traditional route in courting a woman?

In a span of a week or few days the woman you were drooling over on Instagram is now in your bed. The truth is women are putting themselves out there in ways that men don't need to work hard for their respect anymore. Texting sexy or nude pics of themselves. You think that's cute for a man you are just getting to know? He'll appreciate them. So much so more times than not, he'll even share them with one or more of his friends. But, if you're not in a serious relationship with a man, you should not be doing this anyway. Understand that once you press send it's out there. A man you don't thoroughly know owns that part of you and can do whatever he wishes with that information. And it may not be in a way that is respectful to you.

Some men do carry enough maturity and tact not to do this but do you know enough of his character to know either way? So many women have been hurt by making this mistake in trusting a person they don't know enough to share these kind of intimate photos or texts. You have to cultivate trust before so much is given so soon. The fact is that many of us women are just lonely. Loneliness has put many of us in the position of making rushed or bad decisions.

You decide to deal in a situation with a man and you know the relationship or whatever you two have going on with each other is a mess. You stay in it because at least you're not by yourself. That's a horrible reason to stay or deal with a man that you know is a dam mess. But, we women do it. We'll complain about life and lick our paw and be on the phone all types of hours talking about a man and his bullshit that we know we ain't gonna leave or prepared to do something about. But, this is our life and this is how we set things up, right?

Hard truth. Stop putting your friends and family through the nonsense of your situation. If you're going to stay in a negative situation then don't take others on the amusement ride with you. The ride needs to stop and all of us need to get off and move on to something else. We women have to learn to get past the point of complaining and allowing negativity. It has to stop. Honestly a man will only do what you allow him to do. If he's openly looking at other women and a cheater and you keep taking him back, then just admit you have a "seeing eye dog" for a man! If he's allowed to cheat and have you, why would he leave? It's the best of both worlds. He's got his one foot in and the other foot out. Your relationship shouldn't be duplicating the Hokey Pokey!

Stand up for your worth and your respect. And believe me, he can see if you consider yourself worthy. Certain men will take advantage of a woman because her insecurities are so apparent. He will drive your car, spend your money and if allowed to will take what he wants from you without anything in return. It's a hard truth. Desperation allows manipulation. Soak that in and let it marinate. When you appear desperate to the wrong individual, you are a sheep amongst wolves. You are in the position of being hurt, manipulated and played. Don't do it to yourself. Know your role, and realize your role on his "team."

You have to look at your relationships for what they truly are. You thinking you a quarterback and you really a safety! Hello! Believe me, he will look at you like you need to play your position, and if you try to come out of that position, he will bench your ass real quick. It's how the game is played for some men. As a woman, if you don't wish to be a part of his "team" then don't try out for it. Going in, you know the kind of man you're dealing with. Know that during the course of this type of situation, the game may change but the rules remain the same.

Men will rarely change their course of action if what they're doing works for and benefits them. Now as a pro man woman, I'm not putting down men here. Let me be abundantly clear in saying that for some men, yes, they will take advantage of advantageous situations if given the opportunity. But, a man that wants a woman for more than just sex will be very clear of his intentions. He will court you. Show an interest in your life. Inquire about your work and your goals. Ask about your family. He will show respect as well as treating you respectfully. If this is the kind of relationship you're looking for with a certain man than you have to carry yourself in a way that commands him to take notice of you differently than he does other women. There has to be something about you other than your physical presence that intrigues him mentally.

Yes, he has to be physically attracted to you as well. That is important. But, something has to feel different for him that makes him want more with you. It has to come from a place of genuineness. It's not something you can manipulate or make happen. You will know as much as he will know. It's hard for us women to digest when a man is not looking at us as relationship material. As tough as we can appear, inside that shit is devastating. Rejection is a powerful depressant. There's nothing worse than every man wanting you, but the man you want.

Looking at it objectively, do we really want to be with someone that doesn't value us as relationship material? You want someone that is equally enthusiastic about you as you are about them. Someone that follows up and follows through with you and communicates with you. You want a man that can't wait to see you and spend time with you. If you're running a man down, texting him and phoning him and he's not picking up his phone or returning your calls and sentiments don't waste your valuable time.

As I stated in the previous chapter, life is short and we don't have the novelty of time to waste on the wrong people.

We have to treat our emotions with care and protect them as if they were valuable jewelry. Actually they're priceless. I'm not sure if many women are fully aware of the power we hold. What men want is US. What we have, they can only have if we give it to them. We devalue our worth when we sell ourselves cheap. I don't care how great a man looks, how big his dick is, or how much money he has. He still needs a woman to be complete! Because what good is all that if he doesn't have the right woman to share it with? Equally, as much as we complain about them and all the stuff they do wrong, we need them too. Because for everything they do wrong, when they get it right, it feels oh so good!

CHAPTER 11
WAIT A MINUTE

"I think women are foolish to pretend they are equal to men, they are far superior and always have been."
- William Golding

Ok fellas! We're here. As much as I love doting on you men out there, we need to have a conversation before I leave. I've told the women out here all the things they need to do to be supportive of you. How to love you, make love to you, empower you. With all that being said, I need you to be worthy of every reason why we women should bestow all our hard work into you. Everything that I've spoken about, everything that I've advocated for has to be for a man that is deserving of it all.

As women, there are just certain things we need from you also. Like understanding. Understand that we come from an emotional place. We put our hearts and feelings out there and it's not always returned in the way that we wish it to be. It's made us guarded. With your love and guidance can we rest assured that with you, we're going to be protected? It allows us the freedom of loving you without reserve. We can let our guard down finally. That protection is what we look for in a man.

We want you to be mature and about your business. It's cute if you're a momma's boy. We admire your love for her. But, we need you to grow up and not be dependent on her or us. We don't want to take care of a man. We look to you as leaders. And it's not about submission. It's about a strong belief in no matter how strong I am as a woman I cannot replace your role as a man.

Your strength guides ours. And as strong as you can be, it's ok to be vulnerable at times. It doesn't mean you're weak in our eyes. It means you're human. We want to work with you to build something meaningful together. Don't win us over, proclaiming you're this and you have that and we find out you're none of those things. Be who you are. Have faith and security in your abilities.

Your confidence allows us to never fear. We're here to back you. With everything that you convey, follow through and maintain your word. It instills trust. With our trust, we need your loyalty. We need to know that we're secure with you. Your loyalty is a representation of your character. Loyalty is important to us because when the world may not roll with us, you will. Your loyalty is unwavering and can't be swayed by anyone's non-belief in either of us.

Don't compromise the loyalty with cheating and lying. We don't want your lies. It breaks down the wall of trust we've worked so hard to build. We want you to take accountability and be personally responsible and have integrity. Don't blame others or your past for your current indiscretions. Own them and do something about them. And if you're mine, then respect that. We're not in a relationship with you to have someone else in the bed with us. We don't want to deal with a cheating man. It's hurtful and compromises our ability to ever trust you again. It not only affects us as a couple but our family as a whole. If you're not happy or something is hurting you talk to about it.

Communicate so we can solve the issue before it becomes a problem. Don't give reasons why you don't communicate well. If you can communicate that, then you can communicate enough that we have an understanding of each other's wants and needs. And as much as we need you to communicate, we need you to listen. You don't always have all the answers. We need you to respect us enough to value our opinions or objections. We appreciate your leadership, but we need your adherence at times. We want you to view us as equals and contributing partners. Treat us with respect and we'll be the best women we can be for you. We'll support you in your dreams and anything you wish to pursue.

Be proactive with your life. We want to see you achieve the brass ring through your hard work and dedication. We'll inspire each other to be the best of ourselves. We don't want to see you sleeping late, and playing video games all day unless it's your day off. A lazy man is one of the most unattractive and unappealing traits a man can have. How can we respect a man that's not inspired within himself? We appreciate and admire ambition. Not only in your careers but in how you take care of yourself.

We want arm candy just as much as you do. We appreciate a man that dresses well and takes good care of his health and body also. But bigger than yourself, we need you to be a man that takes good care of your children. We weren't meant to be single parents. The job of a father cannot be replaced by us women no matter how hard we try. We need you to step up and take care of your children responsibly. Remember that our daughters look to you to set a standard she will judge all men by. Our sons need you to mold them into men of strength, good character and ambition. Your children need your presence not your presents. They need you to be an active and conducive part of their lives. Be consistent and set a good example for them. They need your time and so do we.

Yes, your career is important and your responsibilities as a man can be overwhelming, but allow us the novelty of spending quality time with you. We don't want to have to beg or ask for it. We need you to see it being just as important as we do. We want to be a priority in your life. We don't want to have to keep reminding you of our importance. We want to feel appreciated for all that we bring to the table for you as well. Just like you look forward to kind gestures, we want that as well. We want our kisses, hugs and kind words of appreciation. Our good sex. No, we want great sex! We want and need your passion. Our lovemaking has to grow as much as we do. We don't want the bedroom to be the bored room any more than you do. We enjoy the small sentimental things. We enjoy your laughter. We love a sense of humor and a man that knows how to have a good time and enjoy life. We need you to be a light at times when things can get us down or depressive. Your generosity in giving your time and your love is a gift we can only treasure and respect.

ACKNOWLEDGEMENTS

Thank you to my parents. Your spiritual guidance and love is always with me. To my sister Cathy, thank you for your constant and unwavering love and support. My beautiful children, Stephanie and Devon. I love you more than words can say.

To my Bella Girl, and Benny Blanco, mommy loves you too. To my beauty, Irobia Allen for keeping me beautiful and always supporting me. I love you sweetie! My nephews Justin Murphy and Brian Griffin, auntie loves you.

To my wonderful photographer, Jason Thomas, thank you love. Thank you to Chris Classic, Mirza Babic, Domingo Nunez, for your words of wisdom and support. Thank you Kat Sparkman for the bling! My makeup artist Chyna Russell, thank you for the beatdown!

To my dear friend and publisher Trojah Irby Morgan. How can I just say thank you? Your friendship, kindness, support and professionalism in helping me goes beyond words. I'm so grateful to you in bringing a long awaited dream of mine to fruition. You've helped me in so many ways, I cannot thank you enough. You will always have my heart and loyalty.

Thank you to all of my family and friends in your love and support of me. I'm humbled and grateful to you all. To all the men in my life, thank you for the blessings and the lessons.

To the love of my life, Isaac Freeman. Thank you for all the good times and for all your love and support of me and my family. You know I will always love you.

SHANDA FREEMAN

ABOUT THE AUTHOR

Born and raised in Newburgh, N.Y. Shanda Freeman was destined for great accomplishments! Her 8 year career as a Case Manager and Counselor in HIV/AIDS Awareness and Prevention services laid the groundwork for her Sex and Relationship advice podcast Man and Wife created by her and her husband, FatMan Scoop in 2007. With the success of their podcast garnering them a viewership of 5 million plus, Man and Wife debut on MTV in 2008!

In branching out on her own as a writer and advice columnist, Shanda created her popular vlog Shanda Says! With her unabashed and genuine advice, she has been a contributor to numerous media outlets such as; Essence.com, AOL BlackVoices, The New York Post, Plus Model Magazine, Straight Stuntin Magazine and Hello Beautiful.com to name a few. In a accomplishing her childhood dream from her love for fashion, Shanda created Shanda Style in 2012. Her career as a clothing designer has garnered her much recognition debuting her first collection at Maryland Fashion week and New York Fashion Week in 2012. In 2013 she had the honor of debuting her second collection at BET'S RIP THE RUNWAY at NYC's Hammerstein Ballroom. She was also the featured designer at Curves Rock Weekend in Baltimore Maryland and POSH LA Fashion Weekend in California. In June 2014 she will be showing at FFF Week in NYC and is nominated for Designer of the Year by PLUS NIGHT OUT.

In combining her love in literary and media, in 2014, she started her own production company, Left Lane Productions. Her goal is to continue publishing novels and audiobooks as well as writing and producing shows for television and film. Shanda truly encompasses today's Modern Woman with STYLE, CLASS, BEAUTY AND INSPIRATION!

Follow Shanda Freeman on all Social Media
@ShandaSays
www.ShandaSays.com
For Contact or Bookings: ShandaSays1@gmail.com

Pro Man Woman

www.ingramcontent.com/pod-product-compliance
Lightning Source LLC
Chambersburg PA
CBHW071704040426
42446CB00011B/1912